The Best of
JELLY ROLL
QUILTS

25 JELLY ROLL PATTERNS
FOR QUICK QUILTING

Pam & Nicky Lintott

DAVID & CHARLES

www.davidandcharles.com

Contents

Introduction

Since 2007 when jelly rolls were introduced by Moda, we have designed more jelly roll quilts than we've had hot dinners! We have published thirteen books with David and Charles... and with each book having at least twelve quilts, this amounts to quite a large number! You can probably guess that we love jelly rolls and working with jelly rolls has been a massive part of our lives over the last fifteen years.

We thought choosing twenty-five quilts for this collection would be easy, but it soon became apparent that it was much harder than we initially thought. All the quilts are special to us, and it became a real dilemma which ones to leave out. No one or no quilt wants to feel rejected.

Eventually we stumbled upon a process of selection, which included a variety of designs for different skill levels, so that the book would be for everyone. We wanted a few from each title so that if someone had previously bought one of our books, then they would still discover new and exciting patterns. And then, of course, there are the quilts that over the years have become such favourites of ours that we simply couldn't even entertain leaving them out! We hope you like the quilts we have chosen.

Pam and Nicky

WHAT IS A JELLY ROLL?

A jelly roll is a roll of forty fabrics cut in 2½in wide strips across the width of the fabric. Moda introduced jelly rolls to showcase new fabric ranges. How inspirational to have one 2½in wide strip of each new fabric wrapped up so deliciously! If you want to make any of the jelly roll quilts in this book and don't have a jelly roll to use, then cut a 2½in wide strip from forty fabrics from your stash and you can follow all the instructions in just the same way. Our patterns are based on a jelly roll strip being 42in long.

IMPERIAL OR METRIC?

Jelly rolls from Moda are cut 2½in wide and at The Quilt Room we have continued to cut our strip bundles 2½in wide. When quilt making, it is impossible to mix metric and imperial measurements. It would be absurd to have a 2½in strip and tell you to cut it 6cm to make a square! It wouldn't be square and nothing would fit. This caused a dilemma when writing instructions for the quilts and a decision had to be made. All our instructions therefore are written in inches. To convert inches to centimetres, multiply the inch measurement by 2.54. For your convenience, any extra fabric you will need, given in the Requirements panel at the start of the quilt instructions, is given in both imperial and metric.

SEAM ALLOWANCE

We cannot stress enough the importance of maintaining an accurate *scant* ¼in seam allowance throughout. Please take the time to check your seam allowance with the test in Techniques (see Techniques: Seams).

QUILT SIZE

Generally, in this book we show what can be achieved with just *one* jelly roll. We have added background fabric and borders but the basis of each quilt is just one jelly roll. The size of our quilts is therefore restricted to this fact but there is nothing to stop you using more fabric and increasing the size of your quilt. The Vital Statistics in each chapter gives you the information you need to enable you to do some simple calculations should you wish to make a larger quilt.

DIAGRAMS

Diagrams have been provided to assist you in making the quilts and these are normally beneath or beside the relevant stepped instruction. The direction in which fabric should be pressed is usually indicated by arrows on the diagrams. The reverse side of the fabric is shown in a lighter colour than the right side. Take the time to read all instructions through before starting work on a quilt.

WASHING NOTES

It is important that pre-cut fabric is *not* washed before use. Save the washing until your quilt is complete and then make use of a colour catcher in the wash or possibly dry-clean.

SPECIALIST TOOLS USED

We use the Creative Grids 45/90 ruler to make half-square triangle units, which has markings that refer to the *finished* size. If you are using a different ruler when cutting half-square and quarter-square triangles please make sure you are using the correct markings before cutting. We also used 60-degree and 90-degree triangle rulers for some of the quilts.

Floral Bouquet

A gorgeous range by Sandy Gervais is used in this bright, fresh quilt with a white-on-white background fabric, which sets it off to perfection. Although only one jelly roll is used, it makes up to a generous single bed size quilt. You could, of course, add an extra border to increase it to a double size very easily.

VITAL STATISTICS

Quilt size: 60in x 88in
Block size: 10in
Number of blocks: 39
Setting: blocks on point, plus 2in border

REQUIREMENTS

- One jelly roll OR forty 2½in strips cut across the width of the fabric
- 3⅞yd (3.5m) background fabric
- Offcuts from spare jelly roll strips for border
- 24in (60cm) binding fabric

Floral Bouquet uses a white background to set off Sandy Gervais's pretty fabrics. We have also made this quilt with a dark background, which looks equally stunning. The quilt was pieced by Isabelle Ramage and longarm quilted by The Quilt Room.

CUTTING INSTRUCTIONS

JELLY ROLL STRIPS

· From each floral strip cut the following:

- One square 2½in x 2½in

- One rectangle 2½in x 4½in

- Two rectangles 2½in x 6½in

- One rectangle 2½in x 8½in

- One rectangle 2½in x 14in (set aside for border)

BACKGROUND FABRIC

· Cut forty 2½in wide strips across the width of the fabric and sub-cut each strip as follows:

- Five squares 2½in x 2½in

- One rectangle 2½in x 4½in

- One rectangle 2½in x 8½in

- One rectangle 2½in x 10½in

· Cut two 15¼in wide strips across the width of the fabric and sub-cut into four 15¼in squares. From the balance of these strips, cut two 9in squares (see **diagram 1**).

· Cut across both diagonals of the 15¼in squares to form 16 setting triangles. Cut across one diagonal of the 9in squares to form four corner triangles. Cutting the setting and corner triangles this way ensures the outer edges of your quilt are not on the bias (see **diagram 2**).

BINDING FABRIC

· Cut into eight 2½in wide strips across the width of the fabric.

Tip

If you enjoy making quilts from jelly rolls, why not ensure you always have some 2½in strips handy by cutting one 2½in strip from any new fabric you buy? You will accumulate an eclectic mix of strips that you can have great fun making into a quilt.

x 4   x 2

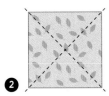

A   B   C   D   E   F   G   H

MAKING THE BLOCKS

1. The blocks are each made up of the units shown in **diagram 3**. Speed up construction by chain piecing all the A units and then all the B units and so on to H. You need thirty-nine of each unit. Keep them all in separate piles.

UNIT A

2. Take one background square and lay it right sides together on a 2½in x 6½in floral rectangle, as shown in **diagram, Unit A**.

3. For the first few strips, draw a diagonal line to mark the sewing line but after sewing a few you will probably find it unnecessary as you get your eye in. Sew across the diagonal. Flip the square over. Press towards the darker fabric and trim the excess. Unit A strips must have the background triangle on the top left.

UNIT B

4. Repeat instructions for **Unit A** but sew a background square on a 2½in x 4½in floral rectangle (see **diagram, Unit B**).

UNIT C

5. Sew a 2½in floral square to a 2½in background square (see **diagram, Unit C**).

UNIT E

6. Repeat instructions for **Unit A** but sew the background square in the other direction. Unit E strips must have the background triangle on the top right (see **diagram, Unit E**).

UNIT F

7. Repeat instructions for **Unit E** but sew a background square on a 2½in x 8½in floral rectangle (see **diagram, Unit F**).

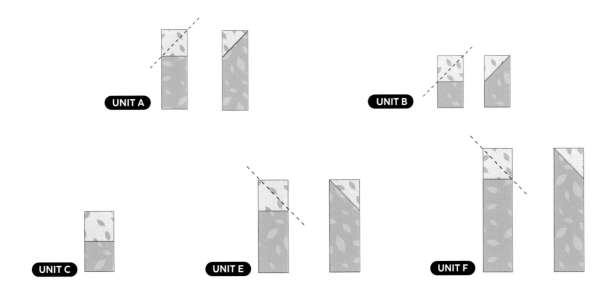

ASSEMBLING
THE BLOCKS

8. Sew Unit D to Unit C (see **diagram 4**).

9. Sew Unit B to the left side (see **diagram 5**).

10. Sew Unit E to the bottom as shown in **diagram 6**.

11. Sew Unit A to the left side as shown in **diagram 7**.

12. Sew Unit F to the bottom as shown in **diagram 8**.

13. Sew Unit G to the left side as shown in **diagram 9**.

14. Sew Unit H to the bottom as shown in **diagram 10**.

15. Repeat steps 8–14 until you have made thirty-nine blocks.

SETTING THE BLOCKS
ON POINT

16. Refer to **diagram 11** and sew a setting triangle to each side of one of the blocks to create row 1. Following the diagram, continue to sew the blocks together to form rows with a setting triangle at each end. Sew the rows together and sew the corner triangles on last.

4 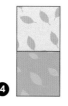    **5**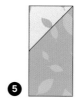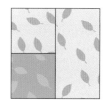

6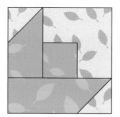

7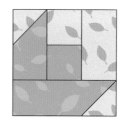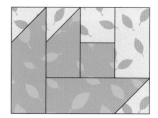

8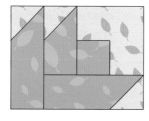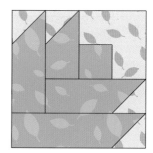

9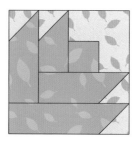

10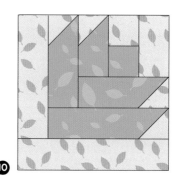

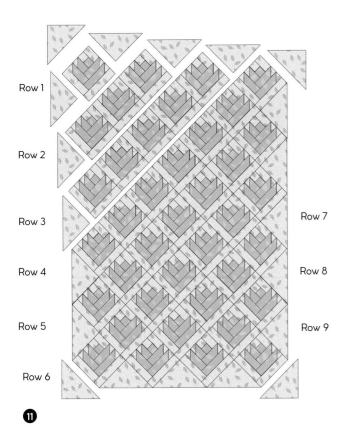

Row 1
Row 2
Row 3
Row 4
Row 5
Row 6
Row 7
Row 8
Row 9

11

ADDING THE BORDERS

17. Select twenty-two of the 2½in x 14in border strips you cut from the jelly roll and sew together to form a long length. Determine the vertical measurement from top to bottom through the centre of your quilt top. Cut two side borders to this measurement. Sew these to the quilt.

18. Determine the horizontal measurement from side to side across the centre of the quilt top. Cut these two borders to this measurement. Sew to the quilt.

FINISHING THE QUILT

19. Your quilt top is now complete (see **diagram 12**). Quilt as desired and bind to finish (see Techniques: Quilting and Binding a Quilt).

 Tip

When you are doing a lot of sewing, have a small rectangle of scrap fabric by your machine and always run your machine onto it when you come to the end of your line of sewing. This remains under your presser foot until you are ready to sew again and you therefore won't have to hang on to the ends of your thread when starting to sew. This will not only save you thread but the tension on your first few stitches will be neater.

12

Hexagon Garden

So many spectacular designs can be created with a 60-degree triangle, and here we have used just about every inch of a gorgeous French General jelly roll to make this quilt. The pattern is created by sewing the triangle units together into half-hexagon units, which are then combined in vertical lines. This means there are no set-in seams required to join the hexagons. It is a really simple quilt to make but you do need a bit of space to lay out the design before sewing it all together to avoid mistakes. You'll be working with bias edges so remember, gentle pressing only! We chose the blue floral fabric from the jelly roll for our border fabric, which ties it all together beautifully.

VITAL STATISTICS

Quilt size: 51in x 53in
Setting: 8 vertical rows, plus 3in border

REQUIREMENTS

- One jelly roll OR forty 2½in strips cut across the width of the fabric
- 20in (50cm) border fabric
- 20in (50cm) binding fabric
- 60-degree triangle ruler

The jelly roll we used for this quilt was a lovely red, white and blue one from French General called Rural Jardin. The bright reds give just the right splash of colour to the quilt. The quilt was pieced by the authors and longarm quilted by The Quilt Room.

SORTING THE STRIPS

Divide the jelly roll strips into thirteen sets of three strips. Each set of three strips will make one hexagon so you can choose how you want them to look. We tried to have two strips of similar colours for the outside of the hexagon and a light or dark for the centre strip in each set. Be guided by what is in your jelly roll. One strip is spare.

CUTTING INSTRUCTIONS

BORDER FABRIC

· Cut five 3½in wide strips across the width of the fabric.

BINDING FABRIC

· Cut six 2½in wide strips across the width of the fabric.

MAKING THE TRIANGLE UNITS

1. Take one set of three strips and sew them together to form a strip unit (see **diagram 1**). Press the seams in one direction as shown. Repeat to make thirteen strip units.

2. Working with one strip unit at a time, take the 60-degree triangle ruler and place on the left side of the strip unit. Place the triangle as far to the left as possible as you need to cut nine triangles from each unit. Align the 6½in line of the triangle with the bottom of the unit and align the cut-off top of the triangle with the top of the unit. Cut your first triangle (see **diagram 2**).

3. Rotate the ruler 180 degrees and cut the second triangle as shown in **diagram 3**. Continue to the end to cut nine triangles.

4. You will have two different triangles – five of one and four of the other (see **diagram 4**). Keep them all together in one pile. Repeat with the other strip units to make thirteen piles of triangles.

ASSEMBLING THE TRIANGLE UNITS

5. Find some space to lay out the triangles into hexagons as shown (see **diagrams 5** and **6**). Select six triangles from each pile, three of each type, and lay them out to form a hexagon, alternating the segments (see **diagram 5**). The remaining three triangles in each pile will be used to make the fourteenth hexagon, the half-hexagons and to fill the gaps around the edges of the quilt.

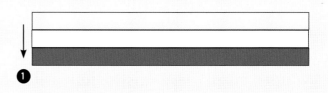

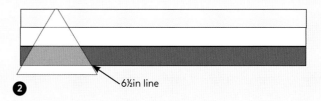

6½in line

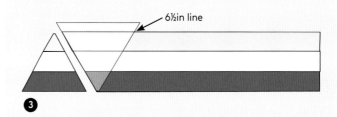

6½in line

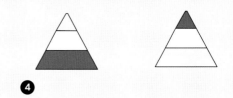

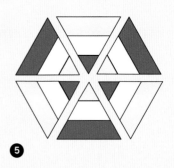

6

7

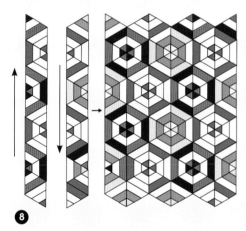

8

9

6. Make the fourteenth hexagon scrappy by choosing triangles from the remaining triangles in the piles. Lay out the hexagons as shown in **diagram 6**.

7. Once you have decided on the placement of the hexagons you can then lay out the four half-hexagons and use the remaining triangles to fill in the gaps around the edges (see **diagram 7**).

8. Sew the triangles together in vertical rows starting with the top left and sewing one row at a time. Pin at every seam intersection to ensure a perfect match. Press all seams in the first row up and all seams in the second row down. There are bias edges so press gently.

9. Sew the vertical rows together pinning at every seam intersection (see **diagram 8**). Press the work.

ADDING THE BORDER

10. Rotate 90 degrees so the top of the quilt is now at the top. Join your border strips into one continuous length. Determine the vertical measurement from top to bottom through the centre of your quilt top. Join and cut two side borders to this measurement. Pin and sew to the quilt to form a straight edge. Press and trim the excess fabric.

11. Determine the horizontal measurement from side to side across the centre of the quilt top. Cut two borders to this measurement. Sew to the top and bottom of your quilt and press.

FINISHING THE QUILT

12. Your quilt top is now complete (see **diagram 9**). Quilt as desired and bind to finish (see Techniques: Quilting and Binding a Quilt).

Double Nine-Patch

A simple nine-patch block is given a new twist in this pretty quilt. We have added sashing and sashing squares and when the blocks and sashing are sewn together another nine-patch block is formed. So if you love nine-patch blocks as much as we do you will enjoy making this quilt. The nine-patch block has been such a favourite over many, many years that it seemed appropriate to use a thirties reproduction fabric plus a crisp white-on-white to create a really fresh and vibrant quilt.

VITAL STATISTICS

Quilt size: 50in x 62in
Block size: 10in
Number of blocks: 20
Setting: 4 x 5 blocks with 2in sashing

REQUIREMENTS

· One jelly roll OR forty 2½in strips cut across the width of the fabric

· 1¾yd (1.6m) fabric for sashing and flip-over corners

· Spare jelly roll strips for binding

For this quilt we used a jelly roll with a lovely combination of 1930s reproduction fabrics, combined with a crisp white-on-white fabric for the sashing and flip-over corners. The quilt was pieced by the authors and longarm quilted by The Quilt Room.

SORTING THE STRIPS

- Choose twenty strips to make the nine-patch frame in each block.
- Choose fourteen strips and put into seven pairs to make the nine-patch blocks.
- The remaining six strips can be used for the binding.

CUTTING INSTRUCTIONS

JELLY ROLL STRIPS

- Take the twenty jelly roll strips allocated for the frames and cut each strip into: four rectangles 2½in x 6½in, keeping them together in piles; five squares 2½in x 2½in. This will make 100 (110 are needed – ten extra will be obtained from the offcuts from the nine-patch blocks).
- Leave the fourteen strips allocated for the nine-patch blocks uncut.

SASHING AND FLIP-OVER CORNERS FABRIC

- Cut twenty-three 2½in wide strips across the width of the fabric.
- Take ten of these strips and sub-cut each into sixteen 2½in squares for the flip-over corners. You need 160.
- Take the remaining thirteen strips and sub-cut into four rectangles 2½in x 10½in for the sashing. You need forty-nine in total. Three are spare.

MAKING THE NINE-PATCH BLOCKS

1. Take one pair of strips and trim the selvedge. Cut each strip into three lengths of 14in (see **diagram 1**).

2. From your six lengths assemble two strip units. Press seams towards the darker fabric (see **diagram 2**).

3. Now cut each of the assembled strip units into five 2½in segments (see **diagram 3**).

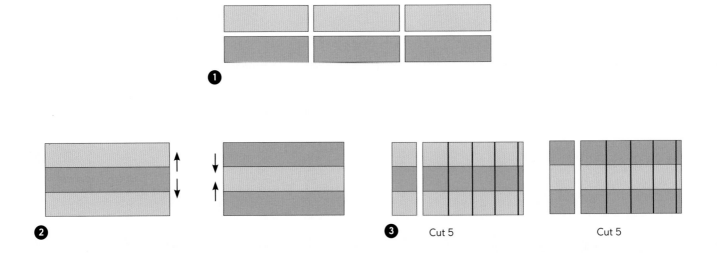

4. Assemble and sew the three nine-patch blocks as shown in **diagram 4**, pinning at every seam intersection to make sure that the seams are neatly aligned. Press the work. Put the spare unit to one side.

5. Repeat with all seven pairs of strips to make twenty nine-patch blocks. Unpick four of the spare units to give you the ten extra 2½in squares required to add to your other squares.

ASSEMBLING THE BLOCKS

6. Working with one pile of 2½in x 6½in rectangles allocated for the frames, take one 2½in sashing fabric square and lay it right sides together on a 2½in x 6½in rectangle. Sew across the diagonal. If it helps, draw the diagonal line in first or make a fold to mark your stitching line. Flip the square over and press towards the light fabric (see **diagram 5**). Trim the excess light fabric but do not trim the 2½in x 6½in rectangle. Although this creates a little more bulk, it helps to keep your work in shape.

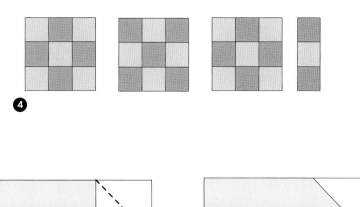

4

5

7. Take another 2½in light square and sew it to the other side as shown, pressing and trimming as before (see **diagram 6**). Make four of these units.

8. Sew two of these units to each side of one of the nine-patch units. Press as shown in **diagram 7**.

9. Sew a coloured 2½in square to each side of the remaining two units. Press as shown in **diagram 8**.

10. Sew to the top and bottom of the nine-patch unit, pinning at every seam intersection to ensure a perfect match. Press the work (see **diagram 9**). Repeat to make twenty blocks.

ASSEMBLING THE QUILT

11. Create the first row by sewing a 2½in square to the left-hand side of four 2½in x 10½in sashing rectangles. Sew together and then sew a 2½in square to the right-hand side of the last rectangle. Press towards the sashing squares (see **diagram 10**). Make six of these rows.

12. Create the second row by sewing a 2½in x 10½in sashing rectangle to the left-hand side of four blocks. Sew together and then sew a sashing rectangle to the right-hand side of the last block. Press the work as shown in **diagram 11**. Make five of these rows.

13. Sew the rows together (see **diagram 12**), pinning at every seam intersection to ensure a perfect match. Press the work.

FINISHING THE QUILT

14. Your quilt top is now complete. Quilt as desired and bind to finish (see Techniques: Quilting and Binding a Quilt). If you wish to create a scrappy binding cut each of the six binding strips into rectangles approximately 2½in x 10½in. Sew them into a continuous length making sure you don't put fabric from the same strip next to each other.

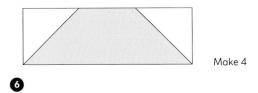

Make 4

6

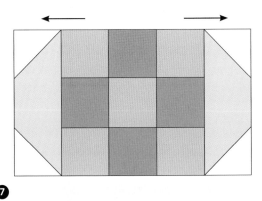

7

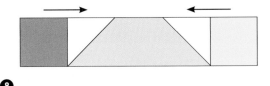

8

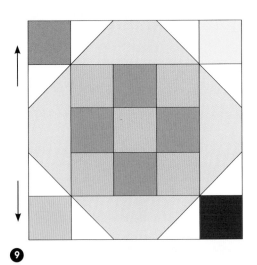

9

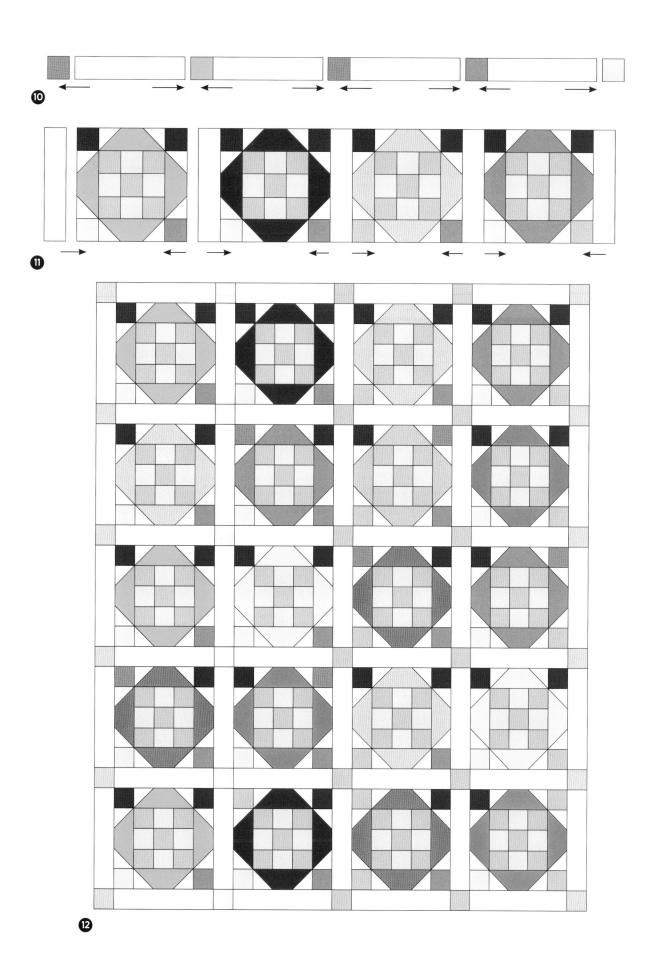

Razzle Dazzle

VITAL STATISTICS

Quilt size: 52in x 52in
Block size: 8in
Number of blocks: 25
Setting: blocks on point, plus 3in border

This quilt is a combination of two similar blocks that look great when alternated. They are very simple to piece although they look quite intricate. For added sparkle we have set them on point. We chose a Moda range called Flag Day Farm from Minick & Simpson, which has a lovely range of blue, red and tan. It was very simple to sort the fabrics from this jelly roll. However, if you have a greater range of colours in your jelly roll you could put different colours in each block. It would create a different effect but that is what makes our quilts individual. Remember to keep an open mind as to colour placement and be guided by what you have in your jelly roll.

REQUIREMENTS

· One jelly roll OR forty 2½in strips cut across the width of the fabric

· 24in (60cm) fabric for setting and corner triangles

· 20in (50cm) border fabric

· 20in (50cm) binding fabric

We have alternated two simple blocks and set them on point to create a complex looking quilt, which is much easier to make than it looks – a good one to impress your family and friends! The quilt was pieced by the authors and longarm quilted by The Quilt Room in a small feather design.

SORTING THE STRIPS

- Choose strips for Block A as follows:
  - Three light
  - Three red
  - Five tan
  - Three blue
- Choose strips for Block B as follows:
  - Four light
  - Four red
  - Eight tan
  - Eight blue
- Two strips are spare.

CUTTING INSTRUCTIONS

JELLY ROLL STRIPS BLOCK A

- Cut five tan strips into 2½in x 4½in rectangles. You get eight to a strip. You need thirty-six (four are spare).

- Cut three blue strips into 2½in x 2½in squares. You get sixteen to a strip. You need thirty-six (twelve are spare).

JELLY ROLL STRIPS BLOCK B

- Cut eight blue strips into 2½in x 4½in rectangles (eight to a strip). You need sixty-four.

- Cut eight tan strips into 2½in x 2½in squares (sixteen per strip, 128 in total).

SETTING AND CORNER TRIANGLE FABRIC

- Cut a 13in strip and sub-cut into three 13in squares. Cut across both diagonals of each of the squares to form twelve setting triangles (see **diagram 1**).

- Cut a 7½in strip and cut into two 7½in squares. Cut across a diagonal of each square to form four corner triangles (again, see **diagram 1**).

BORDER FABRIC

- Cut five 3in wide strips across the width of the fabric.

BINDING FABRIC

- Cut six 2½in wide strips across the width of the fabric.

MAKING BLOCK A

1. Take one red strip and one light strip and, with right sides together, sew down the long side, as shown in **diagram 2**. Open and press to the red fabric.

2. Repeat with the other two light and red strips allocated for Block A.

3. Trim the selvedge and cut twelve 2½in segments from each strip unit (see **diagram 3**). You need thirty-six in total.

4. Take a blue 2½in square and lay it right sides together on one end of a 2½in x 4½in tan rectangle. Sew across the diagonal as shown in **diagram 4**. You may like to draw the diagonal line in first to mark your stitching line but after sewing a few, you may find it unnecessary. Flip the square over and press towards the blue fabric.

5. Trim the excess blue fabric but do not trim the tan fabric. Make thirty-six. Although not cutting the tan fabric creates a little more bulk, it does help to keep your units in shape.

6. Sew a red/light unit to a tan/blue unit as shown in **diagram 5**. Press. Make four of these to form one Block A.

7. Sew them together as shown and then press (see **diagram 6**). You need nine Block As.

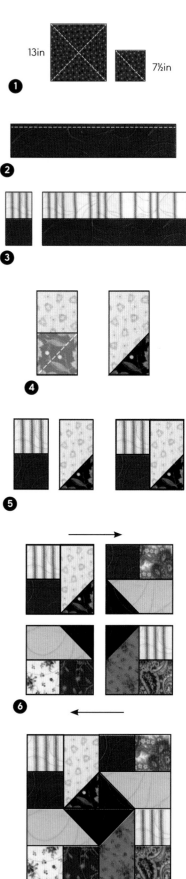

Make 9
BLOCK A

7

8

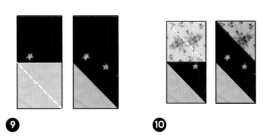

9　　　　　**10**

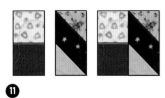

11

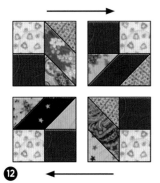

12

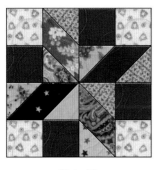

Make 16

BLOCK B

MAKING BLOCK B

8. Take one red strip and one light strip and, with right sides together, sew down the long side (see **diagram 7**). Open and then press to the red fabric.

9. Repeat with the other three light and red strips allocated for Block B.

10. Trim the selvedge and cut sixteen 2½in segments from each strip unit as shown in **diagram 8**. You need sixty-four in total.

11. Take a tan 2½in square and lay it right sides together on one end of a 2½in x 4½in blue rectangle. Sew across the diagonal as shown in **diagram 9**. You may like to draw the diagonal line in first to mark your stitching line but after sewing a few, you will probably find it unnecessary. Flip the square over and press towards the tan fabric.

12. Trim the excess tan fabric but do not trim the blue fabric. Although not cutting the blue fabric creates a little more bulk, it does help to keep your units in shape.

13. Take another tan 2½in square and lay it right sides together on the other end of the blue rectangle and sew across the diagonal as shown in **diagram 10**. Flip the square over, trim and press towards the tan fabric. Make sixty-four.

14. Sew a red/light unit to a blue/tan unit as shown in **diagram 11**. Press. Make four of these to form one Block B.

15. Sew them together as shown in **diagram 12** and press. You need sixteen Block Bs. As in Block A they can be as scrappy as you like.

▶▶▶ *Tip*

You can make your blocks as scrappy as you like but if you want to make them look more uniform lay out your blocks before sewing to make sure you are happy with how they look.

SETTING THE BLOCKS ON POINT

16. Referring to **diagram 13**, sew a setting triangle to each side of a Block B to create row 1, making sure you align the bottom edges. Continue to sew the blocks together to form rows with a setting triangle at each end, pinning at every intersection to ensure a perfect match.

17. Sew the rows together pinning at every intersection and sew the corner triangles on last. Rotate the quilt top through 90 degrees. Trim edges, if necessary, to square up the quilt top.

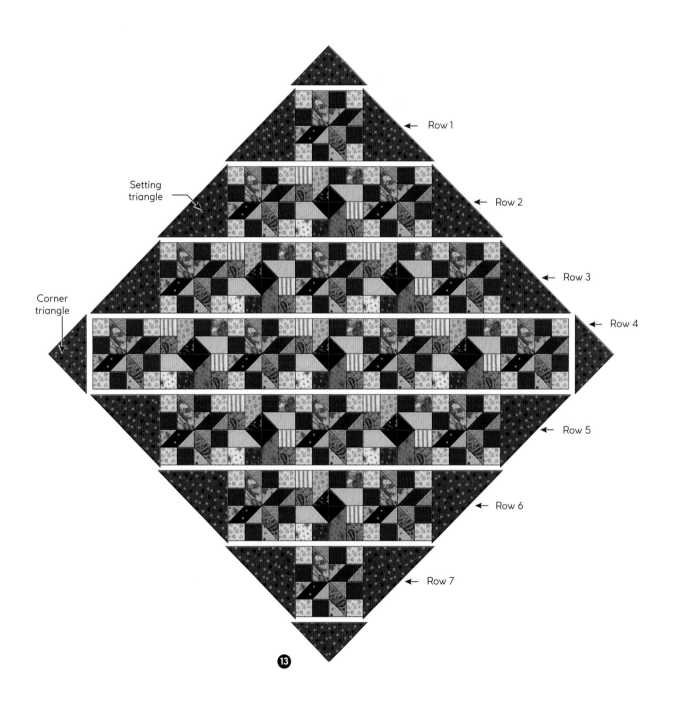

Setting triangle

Corner triangle

← Row 1

← Row 2

← Row 3

← Row 4

← Row 5

← Row 6

← Row 7

13

ADDING THE BORDERS

18. Join your five 3in wide border strips into one continuous length and add the borders to your quilt (see Techniques: Adding Borders).

FINISHING THE QUILT

19. Your quilt top is now complete (see **diagram 14**). Quilt as desired and bind to finish (see Techniques: Quilting and Binding a Quilt).

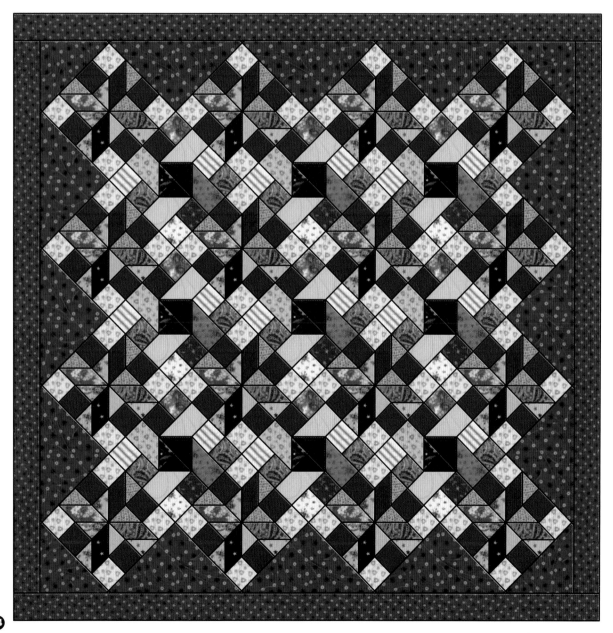

14

Basket Weave

Big, bold and wonderfully modern, this quilt really shows what you can achieve with a few strips and an octagon! You need an octagon shape, which you can either draw yourself or photocopy and enlarge the template we've given. Once you realize how great the octagon shape is we know you'll be temped to use it a lot more! For this quilt we used a 90-degree triangle. Any 90-degree triangle can be used, as long as it measures at least 6½in from the top of the triangle to the base line.

VITAL STATISTICS

Quilt size: 70in x 70in
Block size: 20½in
Number of blocks: 9
Setting: 3 x 3 blocks with 2in sashing

REQUIREMENTS

· One jelly roll OR forty 2½in strips cut across the width of the fabric

· 1⅜yd (1.25m) accent fabric

· 2¼yd (2m) background fabric

· 20in (50cm) binding fabric

· 90-degree triangle ruler measuring at least 6½in from top to bottom

· Backing fabric: 4⅜yd (4m) for an unpieced quilt back OR 3½yd (3.25m) for a pieced quilt back

We used the offcuts from the Basket Weave quilt to make some nine-patch blocks for a small lap quilt, but you could use them to make a pieced quilt back instead. The quilt was pieced by the authors and longarm quilted by The Quilt Room.

SORTING THE STRIPS

- Make eighteen pairs of jelly roll strips of similar colouring (two pairs of jelly roll strips plus two accent fabric strips will make one block). We found a jelly roll with a number of duplicate strips, which was perfect.

- Choose one strip for the sashing squares.

- Three strips are spare.

CUTTING INSTRUCTIONS

JELLY ROLL STRIPS

- Cut the strip allocated for the sashing squares into sixteen 2½in squares.

- Leave the other jelly roll strips uncut.

ACCENT FABRIC

- Cut eighteen 2½in wide strips across the width of the fabric.

BACKGROUND FABRIC

- Cut three 9in wide strips across the width of the fabric. Using a 3¾in octagon template (see Making the Octagon Template), cut three 3¾in octagons from each strip (this measurement refers to each of the eight sides of the octagon), making a total of nine octagons.

- Cut three 7in wide strips across the width of the fabric. Sub-cut each strip into six 7in squares. Cut each of the eighteen squares in half diagonally to create thirty-six corner triangles.

- Cut twelve 2½in wide strips across the width of the fabric. Sub-cut each strip into two rectangles 2½in x 21in. These are for the sashing strips and you need twenty-four sashing rectangles in total.

BINDING FABRIC

- Cut seven 2½in wide strips across the width of the fabric.

MAKING THE OCTAGON TEMPLATE

METHOD A

Enlarge the octagon shape supplied (see **Octagon Template** – it is shown at quarter size so enlarge it by 400% on a photocopier). Do check your full size template is accurate – each side should measure exactly 3¾in.

METHOD B

Draw your own template as follows:

- Using your quilting ruler, draw a line that measures 3¾in.

- Line up the 45-degree marker on your quilting ruler on this line and draw the next side of the octagon at an angle of 45 degrees.

- Measure and mark that line at 3¾in. Continue in this way to draw each side at 45 degrees.

- Once you have drawn the octagon double check that each side measures 3¾in before using it as a template to cut out the octagons from fabric.

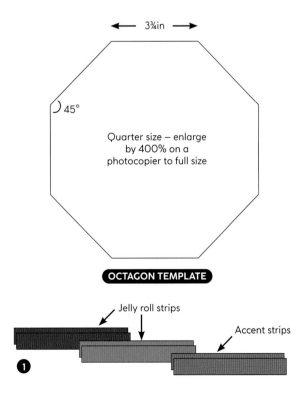

← 3¾in →

45°

Quarter size – enlarge by 400% on a photocopier to full size

OCTAGON TEMPLATE

Jelly roll strips

Accent strips

①

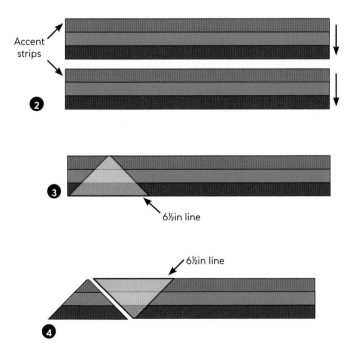

Accent strips

②

③

6½in line

6½in line

④

MAKING THE BLOCKS

1. Choose two pairs of jelly roll strips that are different colours, plus two accent strips (see **diagram 1**).

2. Sew two strip units together as shown in **diagram 2**, making sure the strips are kept in the same order for both strip units. Ensure the accent fabric is placed at the top. You do not want to have the accent strip in the centre. Press seams in one direction.

3. Place the 90-degree triangle on the strip unit, as far to the left as possible, lining up the 6½in line along the bottom of the strip unit and the cut-off top of the triangle along the top as shown in **diagram 3**. Cut the first triangle.

4. Rotate the triangle 180 degrees, placing the 6½in line along the top edge of the strip unit and the cut-off top of the triangle on the bottom as shown in **diagram 4**. Cut a second triangle. Repeat to cut four triangles in total. Note: the remainder of the strip unit, which measures approximately 7½in, is spare. To use this in a lap quilt, or as a pieced quilt back, see Making a Pieced Quilt Back.

5. You should now have two different types of triangles – one with the accent fabric as the small triangle at the top and the other with the accent fabric as the large strip at the bottom (see **diagram 5**). You should have four each of these triangles.

6. Take a triangle with the accent fabric at the top and, with right sides together, sew it to one side of the octagon, but sew only half of the seam (a partial seam), as shown in **diagram 6**. Note: the corner of your triangle will overlap the octagon as shown.

7. Gently press open. Remember you are dealing with bias edges so handle carefully and do not use steam. You will see that the triangle you have sewn and the next octagon side now have a straight edge (see **diagram 7**).

8. Take a triangle with the accent fabric at the bottom and, with right sides together, sew it to the first triangle as shown in **diagram 8**. Press open (no steam), handling bias edges carefully.

9. Now take a triangle with the accent fabric at the top and, with right sides together, sew it to the second triangle as shown in **diagram 9**. Press open.

10. Continue in this way to sew the triangles all round the octagon. When you have sewn the eighth triangle you can then complete the first partial seam (see **diagram 10**).

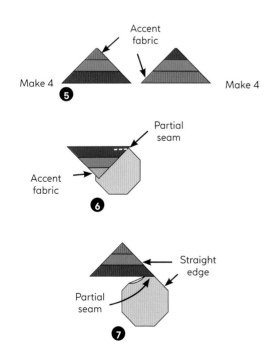

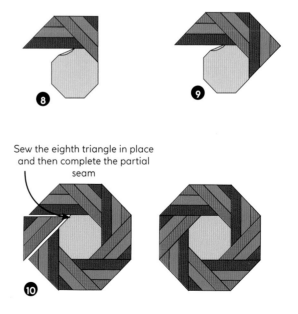

11. Sew a corner triangle to each corner to complete the block (see **diagram 11**). Press the block, pressing seams outwards. Trim the corners to square up the block if necessary. Your block should measure 21in square.

12. Repeat the process described in steps 1–11 to make nine blocks in total.

ADDING THE SASHING STRIPS

13. Sew a 2½in x 21in sashing strip to both the left-hand and right-hand side of one block and to the right-hand side only of two blocks, as shown in **diagram 12**. Press towards the sashing.

14. Sew three sashing strips with four 2½in sashing squares together, as shown in **diagram 13**, to make one horizontal sashing strip. Repeat to make four of these.

15. Sew a horizontal sashing strip to the top and bottom of the first row and to the bottom of the other two rows, pinning at every seam intersection to ensure a perfect match and easing if necessary. Now sew the rows together (see **diagram 14**).

FINISHING THE QUILT

16. You can now make a quilt sandwich as normal with your wadding (batting) and backing fabric, ready for quilting (see Techniques: Quilting). Alternatively, make a pieced backing (see Making a Pieced Quilt Back).

17. After quilting, sew the binding strips into one continuous length and bind the quilt to finish (see Techniques: Binding a Quilt).

 Tip

For the quilting we chose a very popular dragonfly pattern, and to make the design really stand out against the background fabric we used a colourful variegated thread.

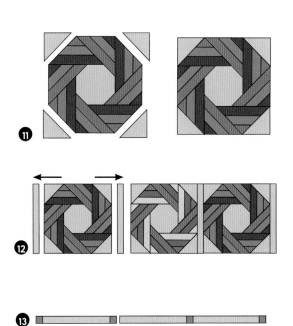

MAKING A PIECED QUILT BACK

The excess strips from our Basket Weave quilt were perfect for making a nine-patch design. You can either use these blocks to make a pieced back for your quilt or use them in a small lap quilt as we did, measuring 39in x 51in with 6½in square blocks. To make a pieced back for the Basket Weave quilt measuring 78in square, an additional border is added all round (see Cutting Fabrics if Making a Pieced Backing).

CUTTING FABRICS IF MAKING A LAP QUILT

· Cut three 6½in strips across the width of the additional fabric; sub-cut these strips into seventeen 6½in squares.

· You will need 1¼yd (1.1m) of additional fabric for the border. Cut four 5in wide strips across the width of the fabric for the borders.

CUTTING FABRICS IF MAKING A PIECED BACKING

· Cut three 6½in strips across the width of the additional fabric; sub-cut these strips into seventeen 6½in squares.

· If making as a backing you will need a wider border. You will need 3½yd (3.25m) of additional fabric for this. Cut two pieces 24½in wide across the width of the fabric for the side borders. Cut four pieces 18½in wide across the width of the fabric for the top and bottom borders. Join the strips in pairs so they are long enough.

MAKING THE NINE-PATCH BLOCKS

1. Gather up the excess fabric from the strip units made for the Basket Weave quilt and cut into 2½in segments. You also have three spare jelly roll strips that could be sewn together into a strip unit and then cut up into 2½in segments.

2. Mix up the segments and sew three segments together to make a nine-patch block (see **diagram 15**). Make eighteen nine-patch blocks in total.

ASSEMBLING THE QUILT BACK

3. Lay out the blocks, alternating a nine-patch block with a 6½in square, as shown in **diagram 16**. When you are happy with the layout, sew the blocks into rows and then sew the rows together. If you always press your seams towards the background square your seams will nest together nicely when sewing the rows together.

4. Sew on the border strips, sewing the side borders on first and pressing seams outwards. Use the narrower borders for the lap quilt or the wider borders for the backing. Sew on the top and bottom borders to complete your quilt top (see **diagram 17**).

5. If making the lap quilt, make a quilt sandwich as normal with wadding (batting) and backing fabric, ready for quilting (see Techniques: Quilting). Bind the lap quilt to finish (see Techniques: Binding a Quilt).

15 Make 18

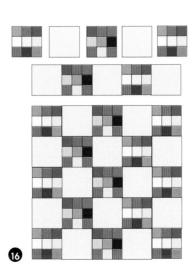

16

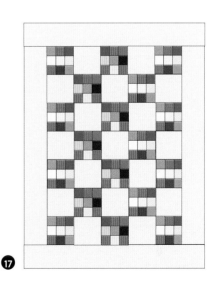

17

Tumbling Blocks

It was a challenge to create this design simply and with no set-in seams. We hope you agree that this is a quick and easy method that goes together beautifully. The three-dimensional effect of Tumbling Blocks is made by the correct mix of dark, medium and light fabrics. We found our darks and mediums in Panier de Fleurs from French General, which gave a good mix of dark blues and reds, plus it also had lots of greys that could be used as our medium fabrics. We added a cream-on-cream fabric as additional fabric, which became our light.

VITAL STATISTICS

Quilt size: 60in x 64in
Setting: 26 vertical rows of 16 units each, plus 4½in border

REQUIREMENTS

- One jelly roll OR forty 2½in strips cut across the width of the fabric
- 1½yd (1.4m) light fabric OR sixteen assorted light 3in wide strips cut across the width of the fabric
- 1¾yd (1.6m) border fabric
- Spare jelly roll strips for binding
- 60-degree triangle ruler

Piecing the quilt in vertical rows means there are no set-in seams and once you get started it really does go together quickly – or relatively quickly given the complexity of the pattern! The quilt was pieced by the authors and longarm quilted by The Quilt Room.

SORTING THE STRIPS

· Sort the jelly roll into sixteen dark strips and sixteen medium strips.

· The eight remaining strips can be used for the binding.

CUTTING INSTRUCTIONS

LIGHT FABRIC
· Cut sixteen 3in wide strips across the width of the fabric.

BORDER FABRIC
· Cut eleven 5in wide strips across the width of the fabric. Set four aside for the side borders.

· Keep the remaining seven strips folded and sub-cut each into eight 2½in x 5in rectangles. Still keeping the pairs of rectangles together, lay a 60-degree triangle as far to the right as you can (see **diagram 1**), and with the 2½in line at the bottom cut a 60-degree edge, to give you a pair of rectangles with the angle in opposite directions. You need twenty-six of each – these are the end pieces for each vertical row. There are two pairs of rectangles spare.

MAKING THE STRIP-PIECED UNITS

1. Sew a dark jelly roll strip to both sides of a 3in light strip to make Unit A (see **diagram, Unit A**). Press seams in one direction. Repeat to make eight strip Unit As.

2. Sew a medium jelly roll strip to both sides of a 3in light strip to make Unit B (see **diagram, Unit B**). Press seams in one direction. Repeat to make eight strip Unit Bs.

3. Lay one Unit A on top of one Unit B with right sides together (see **diagram 2**). Align the top and bottom edges and ensure the seams are pointing in opposite directions so they nest together nicely. It is important to always place Unit A on top of Unit B.

4. Lay a 60-degree triangle as far to the left of the strip units as possible and cut a 60-degree angled edge (see **diagram 3**).

5. Using your quilting ruler cut thirteen 2½in wide segments across the width of the strip unit as shown in **diagram 4**. Stop to check every few cuts that you are still cutting at a 60-degree angle.

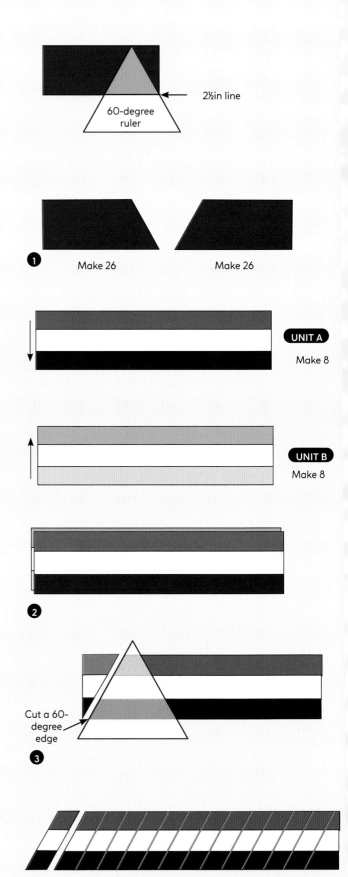

2½in line

60-degree ruler

1 Make 26   Make 26

UNIT A Make 8

UNIT B Make 8

2

Cut a 60-degree edge

3

2½in

4

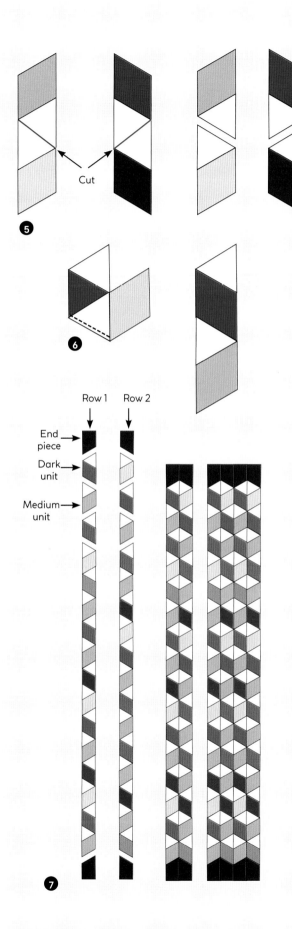

6. You now have thirteen segments from Unit A and thirteen segments from Unit B. Cut across each of the centre light diamonds, as shown in **diagram 5**.

7. Keep the twenty-six medium units that will make the right-hand side of the tumbling block in one pile, and the twenty-six dark units that will make the left-hand side of the tumbling block in another pile.

8. Repeat with all sixteen Unit As and Unit Bs to make a total of 208 dark units in one pile and 208 medium units in the other pile.

ASSEMBLING THE QUILT

9. The quilt is assembled by sewing the units into vertical rows and then sewing the vertical rows together. Note: if your quilt requires careful placement of colours you will need to lay all your blocks out before sewing the vertical rows together. Start row 1 with a dark unit and sew it right sides together with a medium unit. When you sew the units together you will have an overlap at each end as shown in **diagram 6**. Check as you sew that you are forming straight edges to your vertical rows. Sew sixteen units together and sew an end piece to both ends to complete one row as seen in **diagram 7**. Press seams downwards.

10. Start row 2 with a medium unit (again, see **diagram 7**). Sew sixteen units together and sew an end piece to both ends to complete one row. Press seams upwards.

11. Sew row 1 to row 2, pinning at every seam intersection to ensure a perfect match. Press the seams.

▶▶▶ *Tip*

Bias edges will stretch if they are not handled carefully. Just remember to be gentle, with no unnecessary handling and certainly no pressing with steam.

12. Repeat to sew thirteen pairs of row 1 and row 2, and then sew the pairs of vertical rows together (see **diagram 8**).

ADDING THE SIDE BORDERS

13. Determine the vertical measurement from top to bottom through the centre of your quilt top. Join two border strips together to form one side border and two border strips together to form the other side border. Trim to the vertical measurement and pin and sew to both sides of the quilt top (see **diagram 9**). Press the work.

8

FINISHING THE QUILT

14. Your quilt top is complete. Quilt as desired and bind to finish (see Techniques: Quilting and Binding a Quilt).

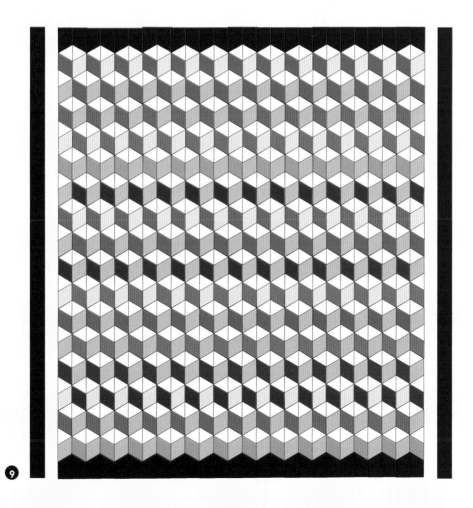

Raspberry Ripple

The nine-patch block works so well with a jelly roll. It's worth noting that you can make sixty nine-patch blocks quickly from just one jelly roll! However, this pattern does something completely different with the nine-patch block until it becomes virtually unrecognizable.

When designing this pattern, we hadn't originally planned to set it on point but we just loved how it looked. This did mean we needed two more blocks so our jelly roll strip offcuts came into their own. We had just enough to make two scrappy nine-patch blocks, which meant we had sufficient blocks and absolutely no wastage. The end result is a super simple quilt that looks stunning.

VITAL STATISTICS

Quilt size: 64in x 80in
Block size: 12in
Number of blocks: 32
Setting: blocks on point

REQUIREMENTS

- One jelly roll OR forty 2½in strips cut across the width of the fabric
- 2¼yd (2m) background fabric
- 1½yd (1.4m) fabric for setting triangles
- 24in (60cm) binding fabric
- Quilting square

This quilt would not be easily recognized as being made from a nine-patch block but that is how it started out! We thought the quilt looked very romantic so we decided upon a heart design for the quilting. The quilt was pieced by the authors and longarm quilted by The Quilt Room.

CUTTING INSTRUCTIONS

BACKGROUND FABRIC

· Cut eleven 6½in wide strips across the width of the fabric.

· Sub-cut each strip into six squares 6½in x 6½in. You need sixty-four in total (two are spare).

SETTING TRIANGLES FABRIC

· Cut two 19in wide strips across the width of the fabric. Sub-cut each into two squares 19in x 19in.

· Cut across both diagonals of each square to create sixteen setting triangles (two are spare).

· Cut one strip 11in wide strip across the width of the fabric. Sub-cut this strip into two squares 11in x 11in.

· Cut across one diagonal of each square to create four corner triangles. Cutting the setting and corner triangles in this way ensures that there are no bias edges on the outside of your quilt.

BINDING FABRIC

· Cut eight 2½in wide strips across the width of the fabric.

MAKING THE NINE-PATCH BLOCKS

1. Pair up the forty jelly roll strips. Take one pair and trim the selvedge. Cut each into three lengths of approximately 14in. From your six lengths assemble two-strip segments. Press seams to the darker fabric (see **diagram 1**).

2. Now cut each into five 2½in segments (see **diagram 2**).

3. Assemble and sew the three nine-patch blocks as shown in **diagram 3**, pinning at every intersection to make sure that the seams are neatly aligned. Press and put the spare unit to one side.

4. Repeat with other sets of strips to make sixty nine-patch blocks.

5. Choose twelve of the spare units and make up four more scrappy nine-patch blocks. You need sixty-four nine-patch blocks in total.

6. Take one of the 6½in background squares and on the wrong side draw a line across one of the diagonals, as shown in **diagram 4**.

7. With right sides together, lay the marked background square on top of one of the nine-patch blocks, aligning the edges. Sew a ¼in seam on both sides of the marked diagonal (see **diagram 5**).

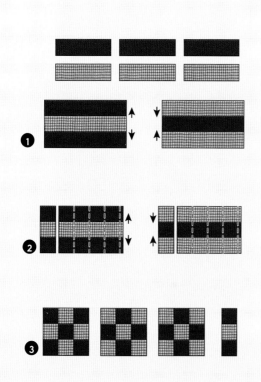

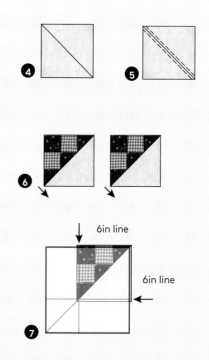

8. Press the stitching line to set the stitches. Cut the units apart between the stitching, cutting on the marked line. Trim dog ears and press open towards the background fabric to create two new units (see **diagram 6**).

9. Using a quilting square, trim the units to measure 6in square. Make sure the diagonal markings on the quilting square align with the diagonal of the unit. You will need to trim two sides and then rotate the square to trim the other two sides (see **diagram 7**). Repeat with the remaining sixty-three background and nine-patch units to create a total of 128 units.

ASSEMBLING THE BLOCKS

10. The quilt is made up of two blocks, both formed from four of the units – a pinwheel block and a diamond block (see **diagram 8**).

11. Make up twenty pinwheel blocks and twelve diamond blocks, pinning at every intersection to ensure a perfect fit. They can be as scrappy or as coordinated as you like. Press, trying to ensure that you are pressing seams in different directions to create less bulk.

SETTING THE BLOCKS ON POINT

12. Referring to **diagram 9**, sew a setting triangle to each side of a pinwheel block to create row 1. The setting triangles have been cut slightly larger to make the blocks 'float', so when sewing the setting triangles make sure that the bottom of the triangle is aligned with the block. Press seams as shown.

13. Following **diagram 10**, continue to sew the blocks together to form rows with setting triangles at each end. Pin at every intersection to ensure a perfect match. Press, trying to ensure that you are pressing the seams in different directions on alternate rows so that seams nest together nicely.

14. Sew the rows together, pinning at every intersection, and sew the corner triangles on last.

FINISHING THE QUILT

15. Your quilt top is complete. Quilt as desired and bind to finish (see Techniques: Quilting and Binding a Quilt).

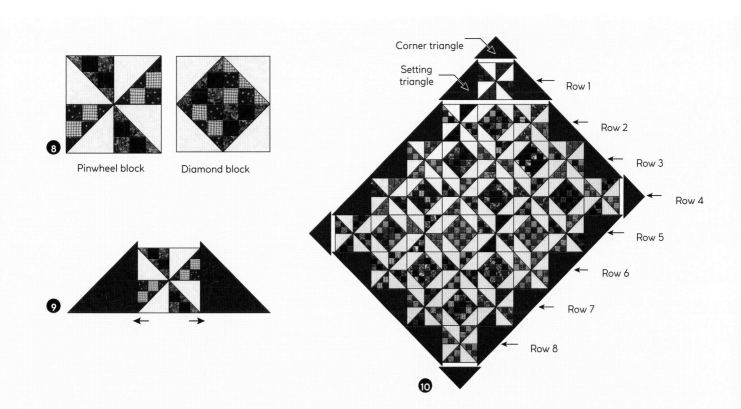

Pinwheel block   Diamond block

Corner triangle

Setting triangle

Row 1
Row 2
Row 3
Row 4
Row 5
Row 6
Row 7
Row 8

Beach Life

VITAL STATISTICS

Quilt size: 58in x 58in
Block size: 8in
Number of blocks: 16
Setting: 4 x 4 blocks with 2in sashing, plus 8in piano keys border

This quilt goes together beautifully with no wastage but you do need your strips to measure 42½in. Most strips measure up to 44in so this shouldn't be a problem but just be careful that you are not over-zealous when trimming the selvedges. The sixteen-patch blocks can be made quite quickly with good old strip piecing – what would we do without this efficient technique?

REQUIREMENTS

- One jelly roll OR forty 2½in strips cut across the width of the fabric
- 28in (70cm) light fabric for sashing
- 20in (50cm) binding fabric

We used the bright, clear colours from the Flow range by Zen Chic, with a background white-on-white from the Twist range by Dashwood Studio. The quilt was pieced by the authors and longarm quilted by The Quilt Room.

SORTING THE STRIPS

This is a scrappy quilt and there is very little sorting of fabrics needed. All forty strips are sewn into ten-strip units and at that stage five strip units are chosen for the blocks and five for the piano keys border. You could make it more coordinated if you prefer.

CUTTING INSTRUCTIONS

LIGHT SASHING FABRIC

· Cut ten 2½in wide strips across the width of the fabric. Take five of these and sub-cut into 2½in x 8½in sashing rectangles. You need twenty.

· Set aside the remaining five 2½in wide strips for the horizontal sashing strips. Don't trim these to size until later, when you've checked the quilt centre measurement.

BINDING FABRIC

· Cut six 2½in wide strips across the width of the fabric.

MAKING THE STRIP UNITS

1. Choose four jelly roll strips and sew them together down the long side to create a strip unit. Sew the seams in opposite directions as this will prevent the strip unit bowing. Press the seams in one direction, as shown in **diagram 1**. Repeat to make ten strip units.

2. Choose five of the strip units for use in the piano keys border and cut each into five 8½in wide segments to make twenty-five 8½in squares (see **diagram 2**). You need twenty-four so one is spare. Set these aside for the border. Note: don't be over-zealous when trimming the selvedge as strips need to measure 42½in.

3. Take the remaining five strip units that will be used for the blocks and cut each strip unit into sixteen 2½in wide segments to make eighty 2½in wide segments (see **diagram 3**).

 Tip

Most modern sewing machines have a 'needle down' option, which ensures that when you stop sewing your needle stops in your fabric. This prevents unnecessary movement of your fabric and keeps your sewing accurate.

1 Make 1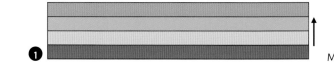

Cut 5 strip units like this

2

Cut 5 strip units like this

3
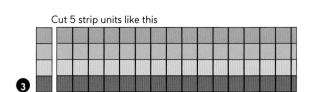

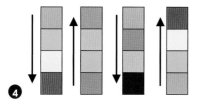

4

MAKING THE BLOCKS

4. Choose four assorted 2½in wide segments and sew them together, pinning at each seam intersection to ensure a perfect match (see **diagram 4**). Be prepared to rotate units 180 degrees if necessary to make sure the seams are nesting together nicely before sewing. Press the sewn seams.

5. Repeat this process to make twenty blocks in total (see **diagram 5**).

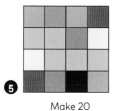

5

Make 20

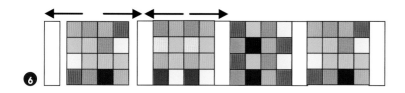

6

ASSEMBLING THE QUILT

6. Sew four blocks together with a light 2½in x 8½in sashing rectangle in between and at each end (see **diagram 6**). Repeat to make four rows. Press towards the sashing strips. Measure the width of the rows – they should measure 42½in.

7. Trim the five 2½in strips set aside for the horizontal sashing to 42½in (or to your quilt's measurement if it is not 42½in). Sew the four rows of the quilt together with a sashing strip in between and also at the top and bottom (see **diagram 7**), pinning and easing where necessary and then press.

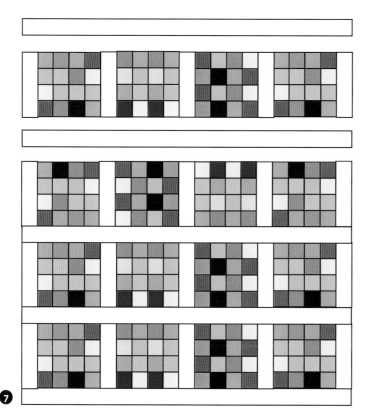

7

▶▶▶ *Tip*

Keep your patchwork neat and tidy by always snipping threads as you go. It will make a big difference to your work and it is a very good habit to get into.

MAKING THE PIANO KEYS BORDER

8. Sew six 8½in pieced squares together to make one border strip. You only need twenty-one segments for each border strip so you will have three extra. Unpick three segments from one end (see **diagram 8**). Repeat this process to make four border strips.

9. Pin and sew two border strips to the sides of the quilt, pinning and easing where necessary, and then press as shown in **diagram 9**.

10. Sew the remaining four pieced blocks to both ends of the remaining two border strips (see **diagram 10**). Press towards the border strips.

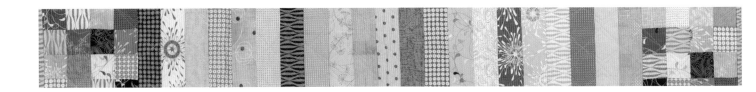

Unpick 3 segments

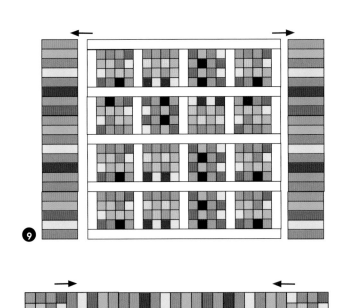

11. Pin and sew these to the top and bottom of your quilt, easing where necessary, and then press (see **diagram 11**).

FINISHING THE QUILT

12. Your quilt top is now complete (see **diagram 12**). Quilt as desired and bind to finish (see Techniques: Quilting and Binding a Quilt).

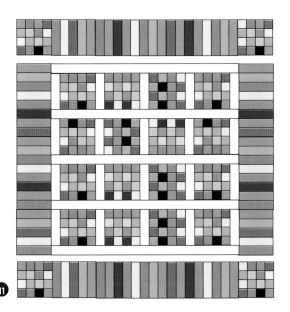

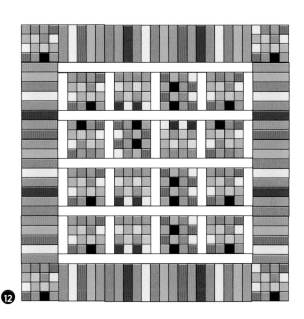

Tutti-Frutti

This is a great quilt to make if you want to use up any odd jelly roll strips you may have. We decided to use up lots of spare strips we had and as long as the strip was bright and colourful it made its way into our jelly roll. We loved the bright, cheery effect and this quilt is definitely one to make if you need to do a bit of 'stash busting'. The blocks each have two four-patch units, which are strip pieced for speed — chain piecing makes the process even faster. The four-patch units coupled with snowball units create interesting secondary patterns.

VITAL STATISTICS

Quilt size: 48in x 64in
Block size: 16in
Number of blocks: 12
Setting: 3 x 4 blocks

REQUIREMENTS

- One jelly roll OR forty 2½in strips cut across the width of the fabric
- 1½yd (1.4m) background fabric
- 20in (50cm) binding fabric

This Tutti-Frutti quilt has a timeless quality, featuring such vibrant colours against the striking white that we used for the background fabric. The quilt was pieced by the authors and quilted by The Quilt Room.

SORTING THE STRIPS

· Choose twenty-four strips for the four-patch units.

· Choose twelve strips for the corners of the snowball units.

· Four strips are spare.

CUTTING INSTRUCTIONS

JELLY ROLL STRIPS

· Take the twelve strips allocated for the corners of the snowball units and sub-cut each strip into sixteen 2½in squares to make 192 in total.

· Leave the twenty-four strips for the four-patch units uncut.

BACKGROUND FABRIC

· Cut eleven 4½in wide strips across the width of the fabric. Sub-cut each strip into nine 4½in squares. You will need ninety-six (three are spare).

BINDING FABRIC

· Cut six 2½in wide strips across the width of the fabric.

MAKING THE FOUR-PATCH UNITS

1. Choose two contrasting jelly roll strips and lay them right sides together. Sew down the long side. Open and press towards the darker fabric (see **diagram 1**). Repeat with all twenty-four strips allocated for the four-patch units to make a total of twelve strip units, chain piecing for speed.

2. Choose two strip units and with right sides together, lay one strip unit on top of another, with the light strip on the top of one unit and on the bottom of another, ensuring that the centre seams are in alignment (see **diagram 2**).

3. Sub-cut into sixteen 2½in wide segments, as shown in **diagram 3**.

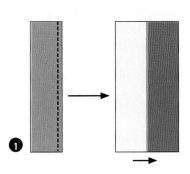

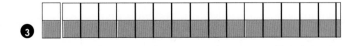

 Tip

To make cutting faster you can layer up strips before cutting, but make sure you don't cut through too many at once or you will lose accuracy.

4. Carefully keeping the pairs together, sew down the long side as shown in **diagram 4**, pinning at the seam intersection to ensure a perfect match. The seams will nest together nicely as they are pressed in different directions. Chain piece for speed. Press open to form sixteen four-patch units.

5. Repeat this process with the remaining strip units to make a total of ninety-six four-patch units (see **diagram 5**).

MAKING THE SNOWBALL UNITS

6. Draw a diagonal line from corner to corner on the wrong side of a 2½in square allocated for the snowball unit corners (see **diagram 6**).

7. With right sides together, lay a marked square on one corner of a 4½in background square, aligning the outer edges. Sew across the diagonal, using the marked diagonal line as the stitching line (see **diagram 7**). After a while you may find that you do not need to draw the line as it is not difficult to judge the sewing line. Alternatively, mark the line with a fold.

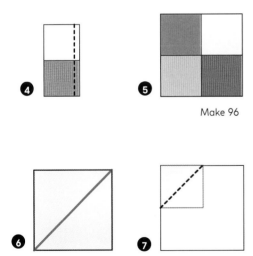

Make 96

▶▶▶ *Tip*

Pressing seams in opposite directions makes it much easier to match seams neatly.

8. Flip the square over and press towards the outside of the block (see **diagram 8**). Trim the excess fabric from the snowball corner but do not trim the background fabric. Although this creates a little more bulk, the background fabric will help keep your patchwork in shape.

9. Now use this same method to sew a square on the opposite corner (see **diagram 9**). Repeat the process to make ninety-six snowball units in total. These can be as scrappy as you like.

ASSEMBLING THE QUARTER-BLOCKS

10. Sew a four-patch unit to a snowball unit as shown in **diagram 10**. Press towards the snowball unit. Repeat with another four-patch unit and a snowball unit. Rotate one sewn unit 180 degrees and sew the two units together to form one quarter-block. Pin at every seam intersection to ensure a perfect match.

11. Repeat with all ninety-six four-patch units and ninety-six snowball units to create forty-eight quarter-blocks (see **diagram 11**).

ASSEMBLING THE QUILT

12. Sew four quarter-blocks together, rotating two of the quarter-blocks 90 degrees to achieve the pattern shown in **diagram 12**.

13. Repeat with all forty-eight quarter-blocks to make twelve blocks (see **diagram 13**).

14. Lay out the blocks three across and four down as shown in **diagram 14**. When you are happy with the arrangement sew the blocks into rows and then sew the rows together, pinning at every seam intersection to ensure a perfect match.

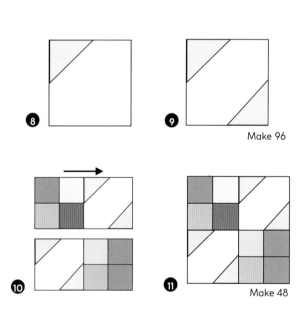

Make 96

Make 48

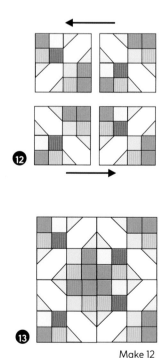

Make 12

FINISHING THE QUILT

15. Your quilt top is now complete (see **diagram 15**). Quilt as desired and bind to finish (see Techniques: Quilting and Binding a Quilt).

Twisted Braid

Who would have thought that this complex looking quilt is made from one simple unit comprising two squares and one rectangle, but it is! We loved Moda's Lily & Will range by Bunny Hill Designs, with its apple greens, pale blues and dusty pinks, but when we saw that the jelly rolls had been split into three different colourways, we had a dilemma! A brave decision was taken and we jumbled up all three jelly rolls and just picked forty strips! We really loved the end result and we hope you agree that it was worth a bit of a cheat.

VITAL STATISTICS

Quilt size: 64in x 76in
Block size: 8in
Number of blocks: 28
Setting: 4 vertical rows with 3in sashing, plus 3in border

REQUIREMENTS

- One jelly roll OR forty 2½in strips cut across the width of the fabric
- 1¾yd (1.6m) background fabric for light squares and setting triangles
- 2yd (1.85m) fabric for sashing, border and binding

If you have a jelly roll that doesn't lend itself to our pattern's split of colours, then just make all the blocks using your strips randomly. Your quilt will look just as gorgeous and it will be unique to you. The quilt was pieced by the authors and quilted by The Quilt Room.

SORTING THE STRIPS

- Choose six strips for colour A (blue).
- Choose five strips for colour B (green).
- Choose thirteen strips for colour C (brown).
- Choose thirteen strips for colour D (pink).
- Three strips are spare.

CUTTING INSTRUCTIONS

JELLY ROLL STRIPS COLOUR A (BLUE)

- Take four strips and cut each into eight rectangles 2½in x 4½in. You need thirty-two in total.
- Take two strips and cut each into sixteen squares 2½in x 2½in. You need thirty-two in total.

JELLY ROLL STRIPS COLOUR B (GREEN)

- Take three strips and cut each into eight rectangles 2½in x 4½in. You need twenty-four in total.
- Take two strips and cut each into sixteen squares 2½in x 2½in. You need twenty-four (eight are spare).

JELLY ROLL STRIPS COLOUR C (BROWN)

- Take seven strips and cut each into eight rectangles 2½in x 4½in. You need fifty-two (four are spare).
- Take two strips and cut each into sixteen 2½in x 2½in squares. You need twenty-eight (four are spare).
- Leave four strips uncut.

JELLY ROLL STRIPS COLOUR D (PINK)

- Take seven strips and cut each into eight rectangles 2½in x 4½in. You need fifty-two (four are spare).
- Take two strips and cut each into sixteen 2½in x 2½in squares. You need twenty-eight (four are spare).
- Leave four strips uncut.

BACKGROUND FABRIC

- Cut eight 2½in wide strips across the width of the fabric.
- Cut five 7½in wide strips across the width of the fabric. Sub-cut each strip into five 7½in squares. You need twenty-four 7½in squares.
- Cut across both diagonals of the 7½in squares to form ninety-six triangles (see **diagram 1**). Cutting the setting triangles this way ensures there are no bias edges on the outside.

SASHING, BORDER AND BINDING FABRIC

- Cut seven 3½in wide strips lengthways down the fabric – three are for sashing strips and four are for borders.
- Cut four 2½in wide strips lengthways down the fabric for the binding.

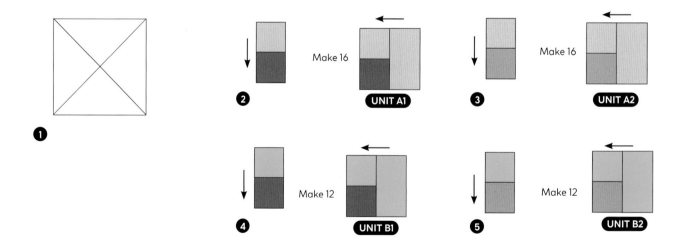

MAKING THE BLOCKS

1. With right sides together sew a colour A square to a colour C square as shown in **diagram 2**. Press the work. Make sixteen.

2. With right sides together sew this unit to the left side of a colour A 2½in x 4½in rectangle as shown in **diagram, Unit A1**. Press the work. Make sixteen Unit A1.

3. With right sides together sew a colour A square to a colour D square (see **diagram 3**). Press the work. Make sixteen.

4. With right sides together sew this unit to a colour A 2½in x 4½in rectangle as shown in **diagram, Unit A2**. Press the work. Make sixteen Unit A2.

5. With right sides together sew a colour B square to a colour C square (see **diagram 4**). Press the work. Make twelve.

6. With right sides together sew this unit to the left side of a colour B 2½in x 4½in rectangle as shown in **diagram, Unit B1**. Press the work. Make twelve Unit B1.

7. With right sides together sew a colour B square to a colour C square (see **diagram 5**). Press the work. Make twelve.

8. With right sides together sew this unit to the left side of a colour B 2½in x 4½in rectangle as shown in **diagram, Unit B2**. Press the work. Make twelve Unit B2.

9. Take one colour C strip and one 2½in background strip and sew together. Press towards the darker fabric and then sub-cut into sixteen 2½in segments (see **diagram 6**). Repeat with the other three colour C strips and three 2½in background strips. You need fifty-two segments in total – twelve are spare.

10. With right sides together sew one of these units to the left side of a colour C 2½in x 4½in rectangle to make Unit C (see **diagram 7** and **diagram, Unit C**). Make fifty-two in total.

11. Take one colour D strip and one 2½in background strip and sew together. Press towards the darker fabric and sub-cut into sixteen 2½in segments (see **diagram 8**). Repeat with the other three colour D strips and three 2½in background strips. You need fifty-two segments in total – twelve are spare.

12. With right sides together sew one of these units to the left side of a colour D 2½in x 4½in rectangle to make Unit D (see **diagram 9** and **diagram, Unit D**). Make fifty-two in total.

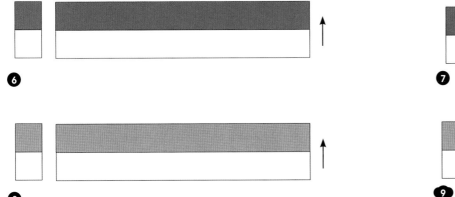

6

8

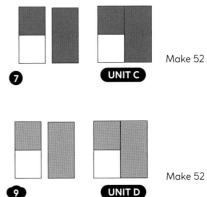

7 **UNIT C** Make 52

9 **UNIT D** Make 52

ASSEMBLING THE BLOCKS

13. Sew two Unit A1s to two Unit Cs, to create Block C1, pinning at every seam intersection to ensure a perfect match (see **diagram 10** and **diagram, Block C1**). Make eight Block C1.

14. Sew two Unit A2s to two Units Ds, to create Block D1, pinning at every seam intersection to ensure a perfect match (see **diagram 11** and **diagram, Block D1**). Make eight Block D1.

15. Sew two Unit B1s to two Unit Cs, to create Block C2, pinning at every seam intersection to ensure a perfect match (see **diagram 12** and **diagram, Block C2**). Make six Block C2.

16. Sew two Unit B2s to two Unit Ds, to create Block D2, pinning at every seam intersection to ensure a perfect match (see **diagram 13** and **diagram, Block D2**). Make six Block D2.

MAKING THE SETTING TRIANGLE UNTS

17. Sew a setting triangle to either side of twenty-four Unit Cs, aligning the edges of the setting triangles as shown in **diagram 14**. Press the work.

18. Sew a setting triangle to either side of twenty-four Unit Ds, aligning the edges of the setting triangles as shown in **diagram 15**. Press the work.

 Tip

Dull or bent needles can snag and distort your fabric and cause your machine to skip stitches, so be sure to change needles frequently.

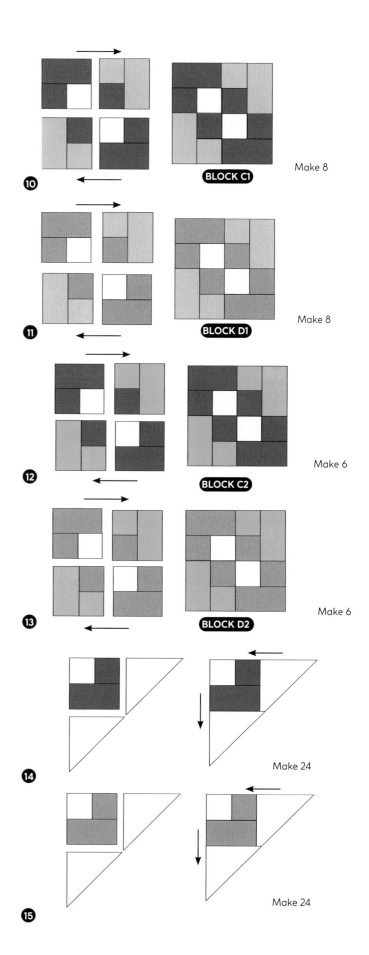

10 **BLOCK C1** Make 8

11 **BLOCK D1** Make 8

12 **BLOCK C2** Make 6

13 **BLOCK D2** Make 6

14 Make 24

15 Make 24

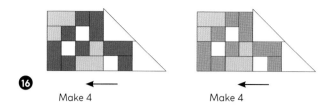

16
Make 4   Make 4

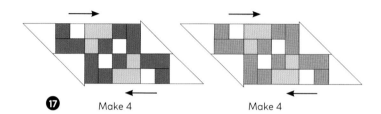

17
Make 4   Make 4

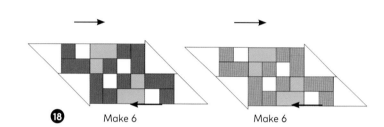

18
Make 6   Make 6

19. Sew a setting triangle unit to one side of Block C1, aligning the edges as shown in **diagram 16**, and pinning at the seam intersections. Press the work. Make four. Repeat to make four using Block D1.

20. Sew a setting triangle unit to both sides of Block C1, aligning the edges as shown in **diagram 17**, and pinning at each seam intersection. Press the work. Make four. Repeat to make four using Block D1.

21. Sew a setting triangle unit to both sides of Block C2, aligning the edges as shown in **diagram 18**, and pinning at each seam intersection. Press the work. Make six. Repeat to make six using Block D2.

22. Sew the blocks together as shown in **diagram 19**, alternating the colours to form one vertical row, pinning at every seam intersection to ensure a perfect match. Make two rows starting with Block C1 and two rows starting with Block D1.

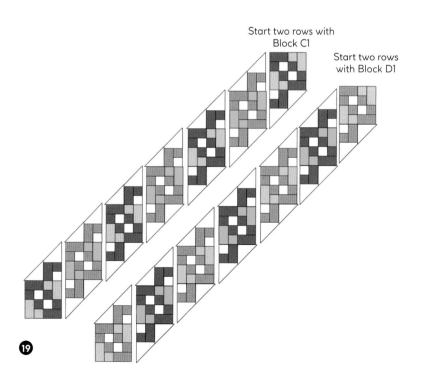

Start two rows with
Block C1

Start two rows
with Block D1

19

ADDING THE SASHING AND BORDERS

SEWING THE SASHING AND SIDE BORDERS

23. Once your segments are sewn into vertical rows measure them all from point A to point B (see **diagram 20**). They should all be the same but you never know!

24. Trim three sashing strips and two side borders to this measurement plus ½in. It is important that the sashing strips all measure the same. It is better to allow an inch or so extra, which can be trimmed later, than cut these sashing strips too short.

25. When attaching sashing and side borders to a vertical row, first pin the centre and ends of both the sashing and the vertical row together as shown in **diagram 21**. You can then pin the rest, easing the strips if necessary.

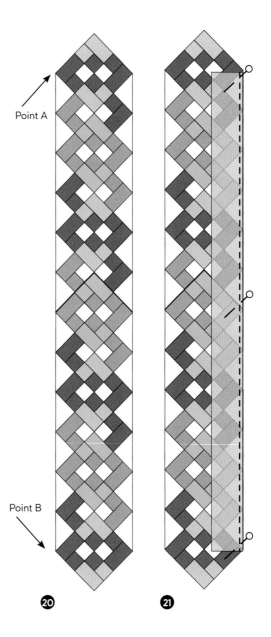

Point A

Point B

20   **21**

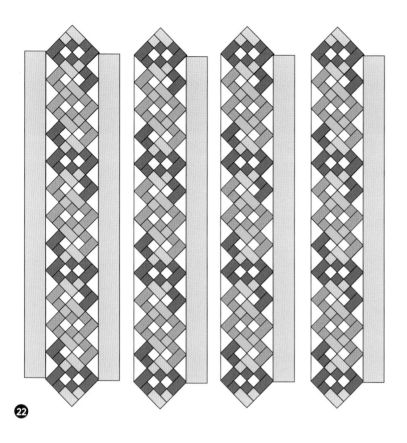

26. Sew the sashing strips and the side borders to the vertical rows (see **diagram 22**). Press towards the sashing strips and borders. Sew the vertical rows together.

ADDING THE TOP AND BOTTOM BORDERS

27. Determine the horizontal measurement from side to side across the centre of the quilt top and trim the two borders to this measurement. Pin and sew to the top and bottom of the quilt, trim the excess fabric and press (see **diagram 23**).

FINISHING THE QUILT

28. Your quilt top is now complete. Quilt as desired and bind to finish (see Techniques: Quilting and Binding a Quilt).

Ocean Waves

We chose to use a lovely blue jelly roll for this traditional design together with a white-on-white background fabric, which creates a wonderfully bright and fresh looking quilt. The design looks complex but it is really just a repeat of one simple block – however we can't deny that there are quite a few half-square triangles to make! If you like red and white quilts too then using a red-based jelly roll would be another option.

VITAL STATISTICS

Quilt size: 64in x 80in
Block size: 8in
Number of blocks: 80
Setting: 8 x 10 blocks

REQUIREMENTS

- One jelly roll OR forty 2½in strips cut across the width of the fabric

- 4⅜yd (4m) background fabric

- 24in (60cm) binding fabric

- Creative Grids 45/90 ruler or other speciality ruler

When set in rows with alternate blocks rotated by 90 degrees, the Ocean Wave block creates a secondary pattern of plain squares, which could be emphasized further by hand or machine motif quilting. This quilt was pieced by Sharon Chambers and longarm quilted by The Quilt Room.

SORTING THE STRIPS

· Choose thirty-two strips for the half-square triangle units.

· Choose seven strips for the extra triangles.

· One strip is spare.

CUTTING INSTRUCTIONS

BACKGROUND FABRIC

· Cut thirty-nine 2½in wide strips across the width of the fabric. Thirty-two are needed for the half-square triangle units and seven are needed for the extra triangles.

· Cut ten 4⅞in wide strips across the width of the fabric.

· Sub-cut each 4⅞in strip into eight 4⅞in squares to make a total of eighty squares.

· Cut each square in half diagonally to make a total of 160 triangles (see **diagram 1**).

BINDING FABRIC

· Cut eight 2½in wide strips across the width of the fabric.

MAKING THE HALF-SQUARE TRIANGLE UNITS

1. Take a jelly roll strip and a 2½in background strip and press right sides together ensuring that they are exactly one on top of the other (see **diagram 2**). The pressing will help hold the two strips together.

2. Lay them out on a cutting mat and position the Creative Grids 45/90 ruler as shown in **diagram 3**, lining up the 2in mark at the bottom edge of the strips. Trim the selvedge and cut the first triangle. You will notice that the cut-out triangle has a flat top. This would just have been a dog ear you needed to cut off so it is saving you time.

3. Rotate the ruler 180 degrees as shown in **diagram 4** and then cut the next triangle. Continue along the strip cutting the required amount of triangles. Cut twenty-five triangles from each strip.

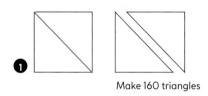

Make 160 triangles

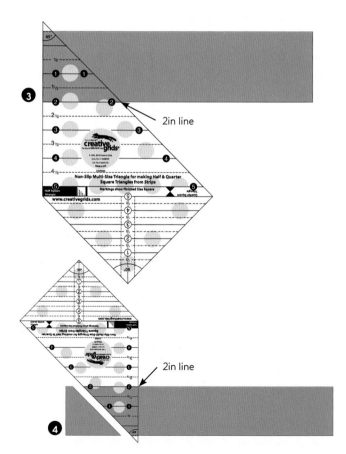

2in line

2in line

4. Sew along the diagonal of each pair of triangles. Trim the dog ears and press open towards the jelly roll fabric (see **diagram 5**). Each strip yields twenty-five half-square triangle units. Repeat with all thirty-two jelly roll strips allocated for the half-square triangle units. You need 800 half-square triangle units in total.

5. Take the seven jelly roll strips allocated for the extra triangles and using the Creative Grids 45/90 ruler cut each strip into twenty-five triangles (see **diagram 6**). You can layer three or four strips together to speed up the cutting process but do not layer too many as you will lose accuracy. You need 160 extra jelly roll triangles in total.

6. Repeat this with the seven background strips allocated for the extra triangles (see **diagram 7**). You need 160 extra background triangles in total.

ASSEMBLING THE BLOCKS

7. Take four half-square triangle units and sew together, pinning at every seam intersection to ensure a perfect match. Press as shown in **diagram 8**. Repeat to make 160 of Unit A (see **diagram, Unit A**).

8. Take one half-square triangle unit and sew one extra jelly roll triangle to each side as shown in **diagram 9**. Sew this unit to a large background triangle. Repeat to make eighty of Unit B (see **diagram, Unit B**).

9. Take one half-square triangle unit and sew one extra background triangle to each side (see **diagram 10**). Sew this unit to a large background triangle. Repeat to make eighty of Unit C (see **diagram, Unit C**).

10. Take two Unit As, one Unit B and one Unit C and sew together as shown in **diagram 11**, pinning at every seam intersection to ensure a perfect match. Repeat to make eighty blocks.

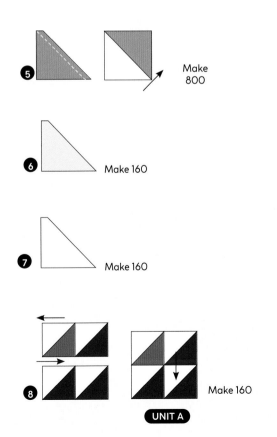

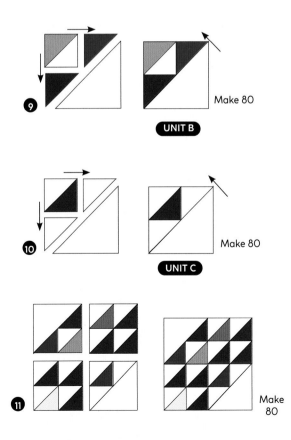

ASSEMBLING THE QUILT

11. Care must be taken now, so familiarize yourself with the block (see **diagram 12**). Notice the position of the two dark triangles in one corner and the three dark triangles in the corner diagonally opposite.

12. Take eight blocks and place them with the corners having the two dark triangles at top left. Now rotate alternate blocks 90 degrees to the left (see **diagram 13**). Do not make the mistake of rotating them to the right – take care with this. Sew together to form a row, pinning at every seam intersection to ensure a perfect match. Press the seams to the right.

13. Make ten rows in total, taking care with the placement of the blocks and pressing all seams to the left (see **diagram 14**). It is helpful to label the left-hand block to avoid any confusion later.

14. Lay out the ten rows ensuring the left-hand block is always on the left-hand side. Rotate the second, fourth, sixth and eighth rows 180 degrees (see **diagram 15**).

15. Sew the rows together, pinning at every seam intersection to ensure a perfect match. Double check all the time to make sure you are positioning the blocks correctly (see **diagram 16**). This is definitely a time for 'check twice, sew once'!

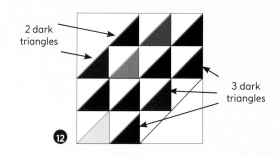

2 dark triangles

3 dark triangles

Move alternate blocks 90 degrees to the left

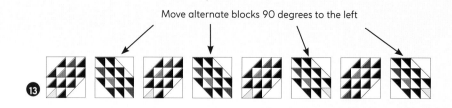

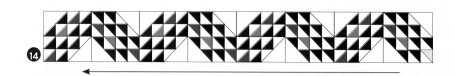

FINISHING THE QUILT

16. Your quilt top is complete. Quilt as desired and bind to finish (see Techniques: Quilting and Binding a Quilt).

High Seas at Hastings

This dramatic bargello quilt is easier to make than it looks as it uses simple strip piecing, plus we have simplified the pattern by creating the design from just one block. The two accent colours help to emphasize the striking undulations that are so characteristic of this type of patchwork. A narrow border makes a nice frame for the design.

VITAL STASTICS

Quilt size: 46½in x 64in
Block size: 12½in x 20in
Number of blocks: 9
Setting: 3 x 3 blocks, plus 2in border

REQUIREMENTS

- One jelly roll OR forty 2½in strips cut across the width of the fabric

- 14in (35cm) each of two accent fabrics

- 20in (50cm) border fabric

- 20in (50cm) binding fabric

Choosing the right accent colours for your chosen jelly roll is the key to the success of this patchwork style. For ours we used an orange and a burgundy. The quilt was pieced by the authors and longarm quilted by The Quilt Room.

CUTTING INSTRUCTIONS

JELLY ROLL STRIPS

· Choose thirty-six strips and cut each into two 2½in x 22in strips to create seventy-two strips.

ACCENT FABRICS

· Cut five 2½in wide strips from each of the two accent fabrics. Sub-cut each strip into ten 2½in x 22in strips. You need nine of accent fabric A and nine of accent fabric B.

BORDER FABRIC

· Cut six 2½in wide strips across the width of the fabric.

BINDING FABRIC

· Cut six 2½in wide strips across the width of the fabric.

SORTING THE CUT FABRIC STRIPS

Sort the jelly roll short strips into eight piles of nine similarly coloured 2½in x 22in strips. Artistic licence can be used here. You also have a pile of nine accent fabric A strips and nine accent fabric B strips, so you will have ten piles in total. Sort the colour piles into the order you want to sew them and then label them 1 to 10. We labelled our eight jelly roll piles from 1 to 8 and then our accent fabrics became piles 9 and 10. Spend a little time sorting your colour piles, as although your fabrics will vary, the design works best when the colours in each pile are similar.

 Tip

To prevent bowing when sewing the strips together, it is helpful to alternate the direction of your sewing. Just take care that you are sewing the new strip in the correct place.

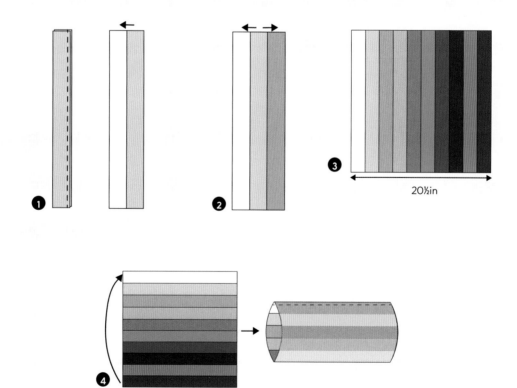

MAKING THE QUILT

1. Take one strip from colour pile 1 and one strip from colour pile 2 and with right sides together sew down the long side. Open up and finger press the seam to the left, as shown in **diagram 1**.

2. Take one strip from colour pile 3 and with right sides together sew it to strip 2. Open and finger press the seam to the right as shown in **diagram 2**.

3. Continue adding strips from each of the ten colour piles, finger pressing the seams in alternate directions. Give the strip unit a good press. It should measure 20½in wide at this stage (see **diagram 3**).

4. Once pressed, fold the strip unit right sides together and pin strip 1 to strip 10 lengthways. Sew together to form a tube, as shown in **diagram 4**.

5. Lay the tube flat on your cutting mat and carefully make sure that there are no folds anywhere. Cut the tube into the segments as shown in **diagram 5**, keeping them in the same order.

6. Take the 3in segment, unpick the seam between colour 1 and 10 (see **diagram 6**) and set this strip aside for the moment.

7. Take the 2½in segment, unpick the seam between colour 10 and colour 9. Continue unpicking each segment in the places shown in **diagram 7**, laying them out in the order shown. Note: when you reach the 1in strip, the design reverses.

 Tip

Reduce the size of your stitch length when sewing the strips together for your bargello quilt.

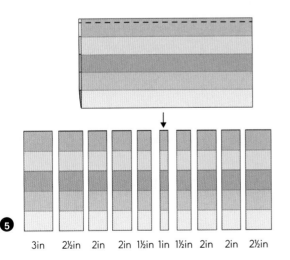

5

3in   2½in   2in   2in   1½in   1in   1½in   2in   2in   2½in

6

Colour 1

Colour 10

3in

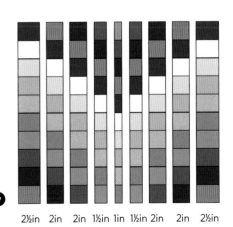

7

2½in   2in   2in   1½in   1in   1½in   2in   2in   2½in

8. Sew the strips together to form a block (see **diagram 8**). As your seams are pressed in alternate directions, they will butt together nicely, so it should not be necessary to pin. Press the block. It should measure 13in x 20½in at this stage. Repeat to make nine blocks like this in total.

9. Take three blocks and sew them together with two 3in strips in between to form a row, as shown in **diagram 9**. Repeat to make three rows. Now sew the three rows together, matching seams neatly, and press well (see **diagram 10**).

ADDING THE BORDER

10. Sew the six border strips into a continuous length. Determine the vertical measurement from top to bottom through the centre of your quilt top. Cut two side borders to this measurement. Pin and sew to the quilt, easing to fit if necessary (see **diagram 11**). Press towards the border fabric.

11. Determine the horizontal measurement from side to side across the centre of the quilt. Cut two border strips to this measurement. Pin and sew to the top and bottom of the quilt (again, see **diagram 11**). Press towards the border fabric.

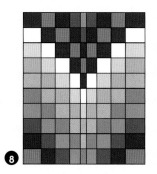

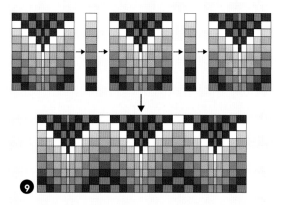

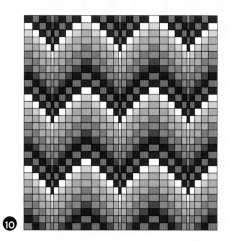

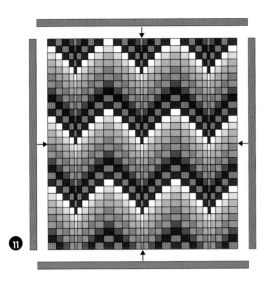

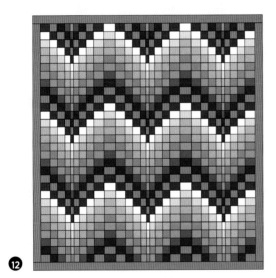

FINISHING THE QUILT

12. Your quilt top is now complete (see **diagram 12**). Quilt as desired and bind to finish (see Techniques: Quilting and Binding a Quilt).

Cloudburst

For this striking quilt we chose one of the colourful ranges by Bonnie & Camille and mixed it with the fabulous Grunge Basics in grey from Moda. The tilted blocks give the quilt a great sense of movement and the colours would suit any modern decor. It is a quick and easy quilt to piece and the excess fabric from the pieced strip units worked perfectly for the quilt back. In the end we couldn't decide exactly which side of the quilt we preferred!

VITAL STATISTICS

Quilt size: 68in x 68in
Block size: 9in
Number of blocks: 36
Setting: 6 x 6 blocks with 2in sashing

REQUIREMENTS

For quilt top:

· One jelly roll OR forty 2½in strips cut across the width of the fabric

· 6yd (5.75m) background fabric

· 20in (50cm) binding fabric

· 9½in quilting square (optional)

For pieced quilt back:

· 2¼yd (2m) backing fabric

· Thirty-six excess rectangles from quilt top, each about 6½in x 16in

It looks as though you need a lot of background fabric for the quilt top but this is also used to piece the quilt back! This quilt was pieced by the authors and longarm quilted by The Quilt Room.

SORTING THE STRIPS

· Choose thirty-six strips for the blocks.

· Choose four strips for the sashing squares.

CUTTING INSTRUCTIONS

JELLY ROLL STRIPS

· Take the four jelly roll strips allocated for the sashing squares and cut into forty-nine 2½in squares.

· Leave the remaining thirty-six strips uncut.

BACKGROUND FABRIC

· Cut thirty-six 4½in wide strips across the width of the fabric.

· Cut twenty-one 2½in wide strips across the width of the fabric and sub-cut each strip into four rectangles 2½in x 9½in to make eighty-four sashing strips.

BINDING FABRIC

· Cut seven 2½in wide strips across the width of the fabric.

MAKING THE BLOCKS

1. Sew one 2½in jelly roll strip to one 4½in background strip. Press towards the background fabric (see **diagram 1**).

2. Cut the strip into four 6½in squares (see **diagram 2**). Set the remainder of the strip (approximately 6½in x 16in) aside for the pieced quilt back.

3. Rotate the squares as shown in **diagram 3** and sew them together, pinning at the centre intersection to ensure a perfect match. Press the seams in the directions shown.

4. Place a 9½in quilting square on the sewn squares and tilt it as shown in **diagram 4** (see Tip). You can change the angle of tilt if you like as this will only enhance the look of your quilt. Cut around the square to form one block. The excess is spare but we saved ours, as we are sure we can use it in another project!

5. Repeat this process with all thirty-six jelly roll strips allocated for the blocks and thirty-six 4½in background strips, to make a total of thirty-six blocks (see **diagram 5**).

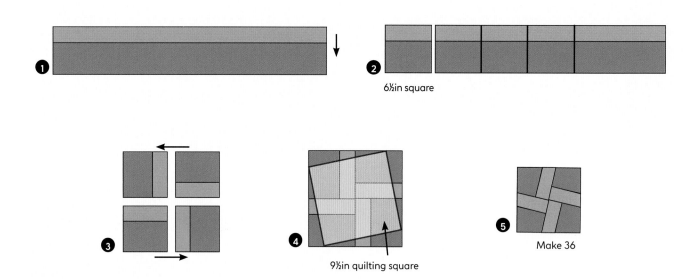

6½in square

9½in quilting square

Make 36

ADDING THE SASHING

6. Sew six blocks together with a sashing strip in between and at both ends to make a row (see **diagram 6**). Press towards the sashing strips. Repeat to make six rows.

7. Sew six sashing strips together with a sashing square in between and at both ends to make a sashing row (see **diagram 7**). Press towards the sashing strips. Repeat to make seven sashing rows.

8. Sew one sashing row to the top and bottom of the first row, pinning at every seam intersection for a perfect match (see **diagram 8**).

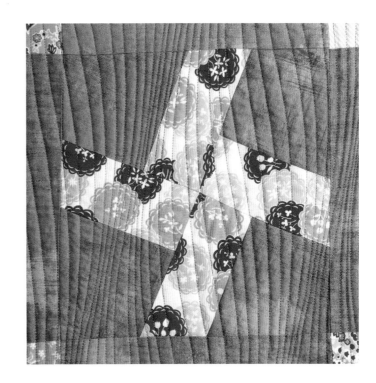

 Tip

If you don't have a 9½in quilting square you can make a temporary one from cardboard or clear plastic – just make sure it is 9½in square and right-angled. Don't use your cutter against the edge of this template as it won't be strong enough to be safe, just mark the shape with a pencil and then use a normal quilter's ruler to cut along the marked lines.

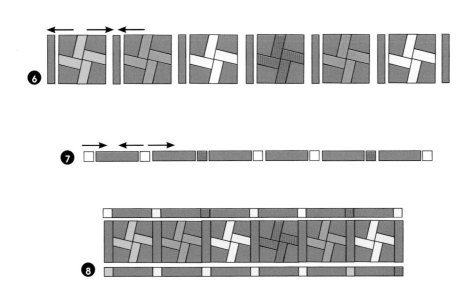

9. Continue sewing the six rows together with the seven sashing rows in between and at the top and bottom as shown in **diagram 9**. Press the completed quilt top.

FINISHING THE QUILT

10. You can now make a quilt sandwich as normal with your wadding (batting) and backing fabric, ready for quilting (see Techniques: Quilting). Alternatively, make a pieced backing (see Making a Pieced Quilt Back).

11. After quilting, sew the seven binding strips into one continuous length and bind the quilt to finish (see Techniques: Binding a Quilt).

MAKING A PIECED QUILT BACK

CUTTING THE BACKING FABRIC

· Cut the following strips lengthways down the fabric (these will be trimmed to size later):

  - Two strips 11½in wide, which will measure approximately 11½in x 76½in

  - Two strips 7½in wide, which will measure approximately 7½in x 76½in

ASSEMBLING THE BACKING

1. Sew the thirty-six excess rectangles (each approximately 6½in x 16in) into four rows of nine rectangles each.

2. Sew the rows together, rotating the second and fourth rows 180 degrees as shown in **diagram 10**.

3. Determine the horizontal measurement from side to side across the centre of the quilt back and trim the 11½in wide backing strips to this measurement. Sew to the top and bottom of the quilt back and press.

4. Determine the vertical measurement from top to bottom through the centre of the quilt back and trim the 7½in wide strips to this measurement. Sew to the sides of the quilt back and press. Your quilt back can now be used to finish your quilt.

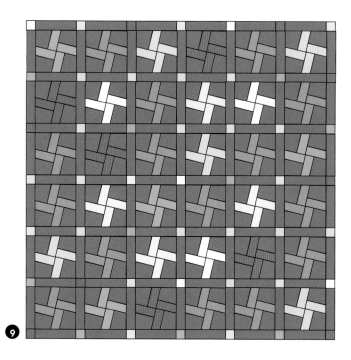

9

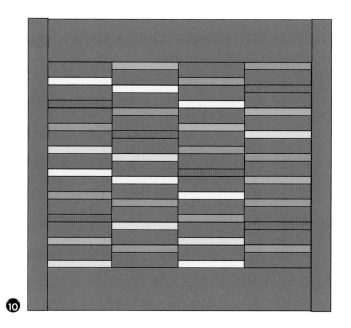

10

After the backing was made our quilt was longarm quilted using a modern quilting design that has become a firm favourite – simple curved lines that flow in and out.

The top and bottom of our quilt back are in fact pieced strips. This was because we ran out of backing fabric! Did we panic – not a bit! We just grabbed an assortment of strips to make up the size. The Requirements list gives sufficient fabric to make a plain, unpieced border. The quilt back was pieced by the authors and longarm quilted by The Quilt Room.

Teddy Bears

The Teddy Bears quilt was made from the same jelly roll used to make the Loving Hearts quilt (see Loving Hearts). Despite being from the same jelly roll these two quilts look very different. We split the jelly roll, using the bolder shades for the Teddy Bear quilt and the more delicate pastels for the Loving Hearts quilt. We didn't want our teddies to be too dark but wanted some brown in there somewhere and this super range from Moda's Three Sisters works well. The quilt has lots of flip-over corners but these are not difficult and the charming result is well worth the extra time.

VITAL STATISTICS

Quilt size: 46in x 46in
Block size: 20in
Number of blocks: 4
Setting: 2 x 2 blocks with 2in sashing

REQUIREMENTS

- Half a jelly roll OR twenty 2½in wide strips cut across the width of the fabric
- 1¼yd (1.1m) background fabric
- One fat quarter of coordinating red fabric
- 20in (50cm) fabric for sashing
- Spare jelly roll strips for binding

The pieced teddy bears on this cute little quilt are bound to be a hit with children and grown-ups alike. The design uses bold reds and browns from the jelly roll but the teddies would look good in any colour. You could also make more blocks for a bigger quilt. The quilt was pieced by the authors and longarm quilted by The Quilt Room.

SORTING THE STRIPS

- Choose six red strips for the clothes.
- Choose two light brown strips for the bears.
- Choose four dark brown strips for the bears.
- Choose one strip for the bow ties.
- Choose two strips for the sashing squares.
- Choose five strips for the binding.

CUTTING INSTRUCTIONS

JELLY ROLL STRIPS FOR RED CLOTHES

- Take two strips and cut each into eight rectangles 2½in x 4½in.
- Take two strips and cut each into two rectangles 2½in x 16½in, plus one 2½in x 6½in rectangle.
- Take one strip and cut into six rectangles 2½in x 6½in.
- Take one strip and cut into eight 2½in x 2½in squares.

JELLY ROLL STRIPS LIGHT BROWN FOR BEARS

- Cut the two strips in half to make four rectangles 2½in x 21in.
- Sub-cut the half strips into one 2½in x 8½in rectangle and two 2½in x 4½in rectangles, keeping the pieces from each half strip together.

JELLY ROLL STRIPS DARK BROWN FOR BEARS

- Cut each strip into seven 2½in x 4½in rectangles and four 2½in x 2½in squares.
- Keep the fabrics from each strip in four separate piles.

JELLY ROLL STRIP FOR BOW TIES

- Cut the strip into sixteen 2½in x 2½in squares.

JELLY ROLL STRIPS FOR SASHING SQUARES

- Cut the two strips into twenty-five 2½in squares.

BACKGROUND FABRIC

- Cut twelve 2½in wide strips across the fabric width.
- Sub-cut four strips into sixteen 2½in x 2½in squares each, to make a total of sixty-four.
- Sub-cut two strips into eight 2½in x 4½in rectangles each, to make a total of sixteen.
- Sub-cut six strips into two 2½in x 16½in rectangles each, to make a total of twelve.
- Cut one 4½in wide strip across the width of the fabric and sub-cut into eight 4½in x 4½in squares.

COORDINATING FAT QUARTER

- Cut eight 4½in x 4½in squares.

SASHING FABRIC

- Cut six 2½in wide strips across the width of the fabric.
- Sub-cut each strip in half to make twelve rectangles 2½in x 21in. These will need to be trimmed to size later.

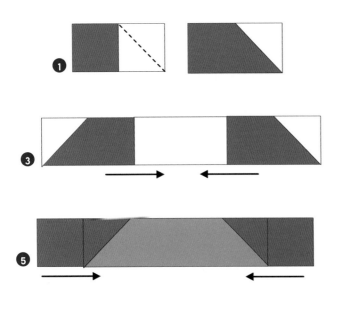

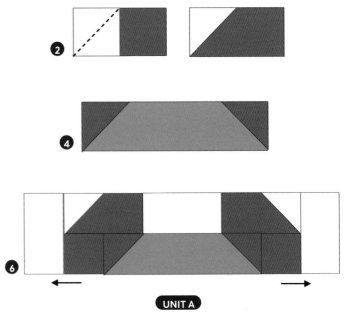

UNIT A

MAKING A TEDDY BEAR BLOCK

1. For each block work with one pile of light brown and one pile of dark brown strips plus an assortment of reds.

UNIT A

2. Take one 2½in background square and lay it right sides together on a 2½in x 4½in dark brown rectangle. Sew across the diagonal (see **diagram 1**). If it helps, draw the diagonal line in first or make a fold to mark the stitching line. Flip the square over and press towards the background fabric; trim the excess background fabric.

3. Take another 2½in background square and sew it to a second dark brown rectangle on the opposite side, as shown in **diagram 2**.

4. Sew these two units to either side of a 2½in x 4½in background rectangle. Press as shown in **diagram 3**.

5. Take two dark brown 2½in squares and using the same flip and sew method as before sew them to both ends of a light brown 2½in x 8½in rectangle (see **diagram 4**). Press and trim the dark brown excess fabric.

6. Sew a 2½in dark brown square to both ends. Press away from the dark brown square (see **diagram 5**).

7. Sew these two units together, pinning at every seam intersection to ensure a perfect match. Sew a 2½in x 4½in background rectangle to both sides to form Unit A (see **diagram 6, Unit A**). Press as shown.

UNIT B

8. Using the same flip and sew method as before, sew a 2½in background square to two light brown 2½in x 4½in rectangles (see **diagram 7**). Press and trim excess background fabric.

9. Using the same flip and sew method, sew two 2½in bow tie squares to the bottom of two dark brown 2½in x 4½in rectangles (see **diagram 8**). Press and trim the excess bow tie fabric. Sew the rectangles together and press.

10. Sew these units together with a 4½in background square at each end to form Unit B. Press as shown in **diagram 9, Unit B**.

UNIT C

11. Using the same flip and sew method, sew two 2½in bow tie squares to the top of two dark brown 2½in x 4½in rectangles as shown in **diagram 10**. Press and trim the excess bow tie fabric. Sew the rectangles together.

12. Using the same flip and sew method, sew two 2½in background squares to both ends of two red 2½in x 4½in rectangles as shown in **diagram 11**. Press and trim the excess background fabric.

13. Assemble Unit C by sewing these units together with the 4½in red squares as shown in **diagram 12, Unit C**. Press as shown.

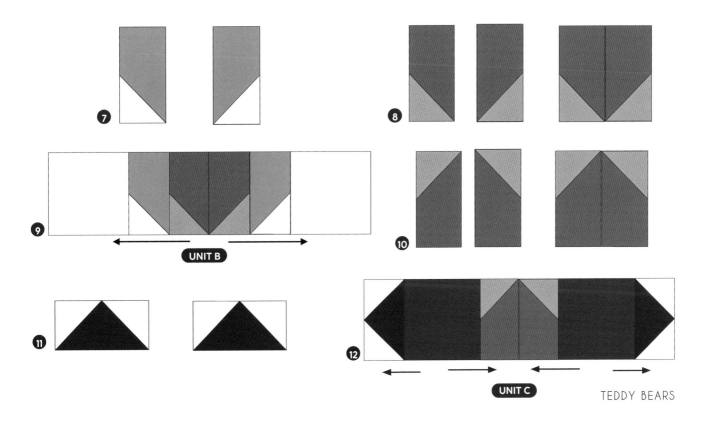

UNIT D

14. Using the same flip and sew method, sew a 2½in background square to one end of two red 2½in x 4½in rectangles as shown in **diagram 13**. Press and trim the excess background fabric.

15. Using the same flip and sew method, sew two 2½in red squares to both ends of a dark brown 2½in x 4½in rectangle as shown in **diagram 14**. Press and trim the excess red fabric.

16. Assemble Unit D by sewing these units together as shown in **diagram 15, Unit D** and sewing a 2½in background square to both ends. Press as shown.

UNIT E

17. Using the same flip and sew method, sew two 2½in background squares to both ends of two red 2½in x 6½in rectangles as shown in **diagram 16**. Press and trim the excess background fabric.

18. Assemble Unit E as shown in **diagram 17, Unit E**, sewing the units to both sides of a 2½in x 4½in background rectangle and then sewing a red 2½in x 16½in rectangle to the top.

ASSEMBLING THE BLOCK

19. Sew Units A, B, C, D and E together to make the teddy bear block as shown in **diagram 18**, pinning at every seam intersection to ensure a perfect match. Press the work.

20. Sew a 2½in sashing square to one end of a 2½in x 16½in background rectangle. Repeat and sew one to either side of the block. Sew a sashing square to both sides of a 2½in x 16½in background rectangle and sew to the bottom of the block (see **diagram 19**). Repeat to make four teddy bear blocks.

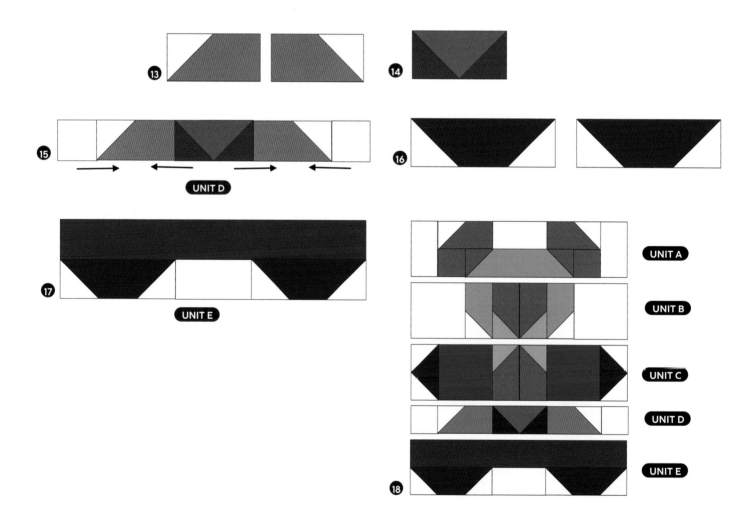

ASSEMBLING THE QUILT

21. Measure the teddy bear block – it should be 20½in square. Trim your sashing strips to this size or the size of your block if it differs. Sew two sashing strips with a sashing square in the centre and a sashing square at both ends (see **diagram 20**). Make three of these.

22. Sew two teddy bear blocks with a sashing strip in the centre and a sashing strip on either side, pinning and easing if necessary (see **diagram 21**). Repeat this sashing with the other two teddy bear blocks.

23. Now sew your quilt together as shown in **diagram 22**, pinning and easing if necessary.

24. Embroider eyes and noses on your bears, or do as we did and appliqué small circles approximately 1¾in in diameter (see Tip). Buttons would not be recommended for a child's quilt.

FINISHING THE QUILT

25. Your quilt top is now complete. Quilt as desired and bind to finish (see Techniques: Quilting and Binding a Quilt). To make a scrappy binding, cut each of the five jelly roll strips allocated for the binding into four rectangles 2½in x 10½in. Sew them together in a continuous length, alternating the fabrics.

▶▶▶ *Tip*

We have attached the teddy bears' small circle eyes using fusible web. Trace the circles onto the paper side of the fusible web and cut out around each shape. Iron the fusible web onto the wrong side of your chosen fabric, paper side up, and cut out accurately. When cool, peel off the backing paper and position on the blocks. Press with a hot iron to fuse in place and sew around the edges to secure.

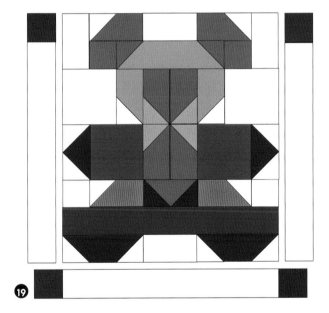

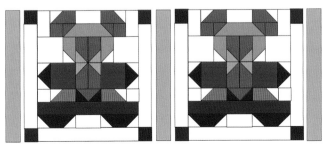

Loving Hearts

The Loving Hearts quilt is a wonderful way to show someone how much you care. With its subtle colouring, you may find it hard to believe that it was created from the same jelly roll as the Teddy Bears quilt (see Teddy Bears). It would make the perfect present for a loved one, and just about any colours would work well. We set the blocks on point with narrow sashing strips to make the hearts stand out.

VITAL STATISTICS

Quilt size: 49in x 49in
Block size: 10in
Number of blocks: 13
Setting: blocks on point, with each having a ¾in frame

REQUIREMENTS

- Half a jelly roll OR twenty 2½in wide strips cut across the width of the fabric

- 16in (40cm) fabric for the outer block frames

- 1½yd (1.4m) fabric for background and setting triangles

- 16in (40cm) binding fabric

This pretty little quilt goes together very quickly and would work well in almost any fabrics. The blocks, set on point, are framed to accentuate the hearts. The quilt was pieced by the authors and longarm quilted by The Quilt Room.

SORTING THE STRIPS

- Choose four strips to be the frames of the inner four blocks.
- The remaining sixteen strips will be used for the blocks.

CUTTING INSTRUCTIONS

JELLY ROLL STRIPS

- Take the four strips allocated for the frames of the inner blocks and from each cut one rectangle 2½in x 10½in and one rectangle 2½in x 12in.
- Sub-cut each in half lengthways to create two rectangles 1¼in x 10½in and two rectangles 1¼in x 12in. Keep the rectangles from each strip together.
- From the sixteen strips allocated for the blocks, choose thirteen and from each strip cut four rectangles 2½in x 6½in, keeping the four rectangles from the same fabric together. The balance of the strips (approximately 16in) will be used to make the nine-patch blocks.
- Leave the remaining three strips uncut to make the nine-patch blocks.

OUTER BLOCK FRAMES FABRIC

- Cut eleven 1¼in wide strips across the width of the fabric.
- Sub-cut five strips into four rectangles 1¼in x 10½in to make twenty. You need eighteen (two are spare).
- Sub-cut six strips into three rectangles 1¼in x 12in to make eighteen.

BACKGROUND AND SETTING TRIANGLE FABRIC

- Cut two 4½in wide strips across the width of the fabric. Sub-cut each into eight 4½in squares. You need thirteen (three are spare).
- Cut four 2½in wide strips across the width of the fabric. Sub-cut each into sixteen 2½in squares. You need fifty-two (twelve are spare).
- Cut one 18in wide strip across the width of the fabric. Sub-cut into two 18in squares. Cut across both diagonals to form eight setting triangles (see **diagram 1**).
- Cut one 10in wide strip across the width of the fabric. Sub-cut into two 10in squares. Cut across one diagonal of these squares to form four corner triangles (see **diagram 2**). Cutting the setting and corner triangles in this way ensures that there are no bias edges on the outside of your quilt.

BINDING FABRIC

- Cut five 2½in wide strips across the width of the fabric.

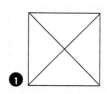

1   18in square

2   10in square

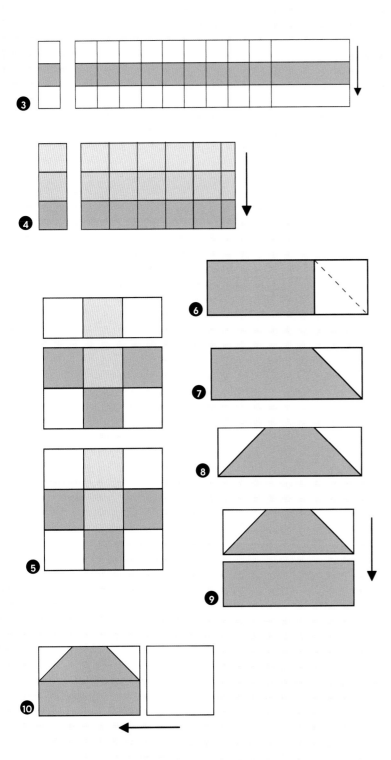

MAKING THE NINE-PATCH BLOCKS

1. Take the three uncut jelly roll strips allocated for the nine-patch blocks and sew them together as shown in **diagram 3**. Press seams in one direction. Trim the selvedge and cut into sixteen 2½in wide segments.

2. Take three of the 16in lengths allocated for the nine-patch blocks and sew them together. Press the seams in one direction. Repeat to make four of these units in total and cut each into six 2½in segments to make twenty-four (see **diagram 4**). You will have one 16in length spare.

3. You have forty 2½in segments in total. Select three segments and sew together to make one nine-patch block as shown in **diagram 5**. Repeat to make thirteen nine-patch blocks, trying to ensure you don't put the same fabrics next to each other and turning the segments to ensure the seams nest together nicely. You'll have one segment spare.

MAKING THE HEART BLOCK

4. Take four 2½in x 6½in rectangles of the same fabric. With right sides together, lay one 2½in background square on one of the 2½in x 6½in rectangles as shown in **diagram 6**. Sew across the diagonal. You may like to draw the diagonal line first to mark your stitching line or mark the diagonal with a crease.

5. Flip the square over and press towards the background fabric (see **diagram 7**). Trim the excess background fabric.

6. Place a second 2½in background square and lay it on the other side and sew across the diagonal as before. Flip the square over and press (see **diagram 8**). Trim the excess background fabric .

7. Sew a 2½in x 6½in rectangle of the same fabric to the bottom of this unit. Press as shown in **diagram 9**.

8. Using the remaining two rectangles, repeat steps 4–7 to make another of these units.

9. Sew a 4½in background square to one side of one of these units and press as shown in **diagram 10**.

10. Sew a nine-patch block to one side of the other unit and press as shown in **diagram 11**.

11. Sew the block together, pinning at the seam intersections to ensure a perfect match. Press as shown in **diagram 12**. Repeat this process to make thirteen blocks in total.

12. Take an outer frame 1¼in x 10½in rectangle, sew to either side of the block and press. Sew an outer frame 1¼in x 12in rectangle to the top and bottom of the block and press. This is Block A (see **diagram 13, Block A**)— make nine of these.

13. Take a light jelly roll 1¼in x 10½in rectangle, sew to either side of the block and press. Sew a light jelly roll 1¼in x 12in rectangle of the same fabric to the top and bottom of the block and press. This is Block B (see **diagram 14, Block B**) – make four of these.

ASSEMBLING THE QUILT

14. Create row 1 by sewing a setting triangle to either side of a Block A. The setting triangles have been cut slightly larger to make the blocks 'float', so when sewing on the setting triangles make sure the bottom of the triangle is aligned with the block as shown in **diagram 15**. Press as shown.

15. To create row 2 sew a Block A to either side of a Block B and a setting triangle at either end. Continue to sew the blocks together to form rows with setting triangles at each end (see **diagram 16**). Press the seams in alternate rows in opposite directions. Sew rows together, pinning at every intersection, then sew the corner triangles on last and press.

FINISHING THE QUILT

16. Your quilt top is now complete (see **diagram 17**). Quilt as desired and bind to finish (see Techniques: Quilting and Binding a Quilt).

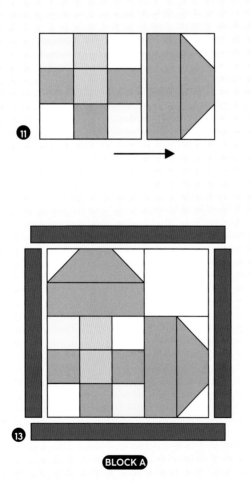

BLOCK A

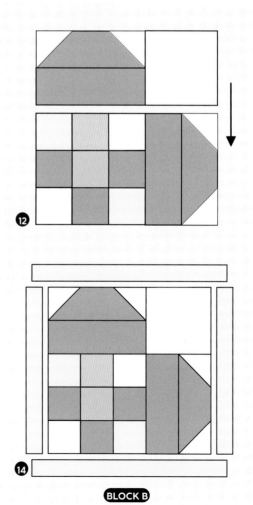

BLOCK B

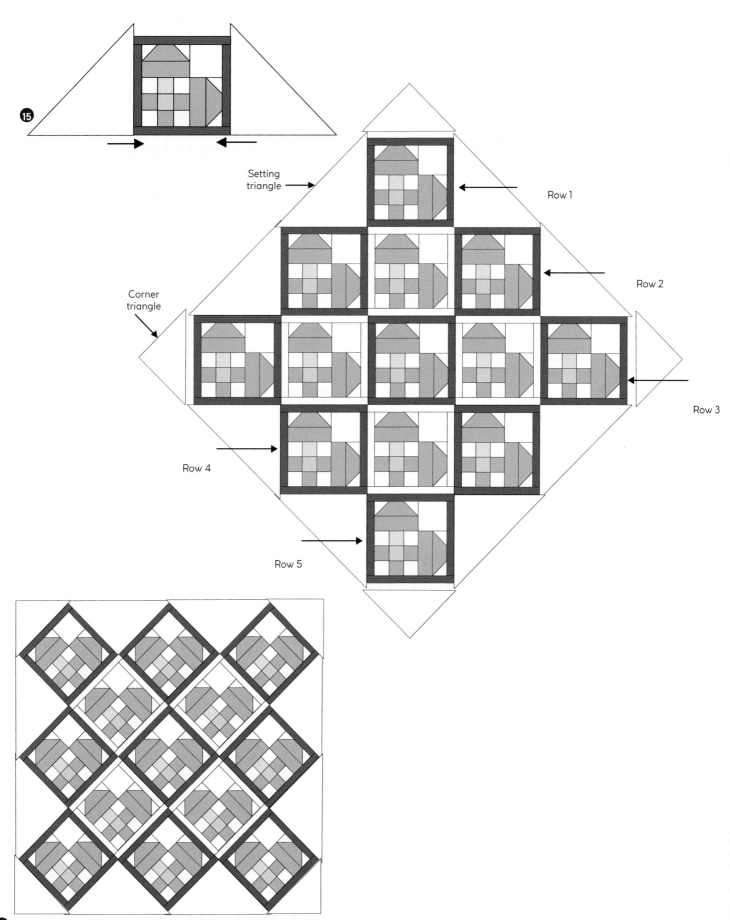

15

Setting triangle →

Corner triangle

Row 1

Row 2

Row 3

Row 4

Row 5

17

Log Cabin Hidden Stars

VITAL STATISTICS

Quilt size: 60in x 60in
Block size: 14in
Number of blocks: 16
Setting: 4 x 4 blocks, plus 2in border

REQUIREMENTS

· One jelly roll OR forty 2½in strips cut across the width of the fabric

· 24in (60cm) fabric for centres and stars

· 20in (50cm) border fabric

· 20in (50cm) binding fabric

When thinking of patterns using strips, the log cabin design comes to mind immediately. How could we possibly leave it out? Any jelly roll could be divided roughly into lights and darks and made up into a log cabin quilt. Here we have added the sparkle of a hidden star. It is not a difficult pattern but the last couple of logs in every block requires a bit of thought!

Our festive quilt is made up in the sumptuous country reds and greens from designer Terry Clothier Thompson. We chose a white fabric with a tiny gold spot for our hidden stars.

The log cabin design is given an extra lift by the addition of the stars. The quilt was pieced by the authors and longarm quilted by The Quilt Room.

SORTING THE STRIPS

Divide the strips into eighteen light and twenty-two dark, or eighteen in one colour and twenty-two in another.

CUTTING INSTRUCTIONS

CENTRES AND STARS FABRIC

· Cut eight 2½in wide strips then sub-cut into 124 2½in squares.

BORDER FABRIC

· Cut into six 2½in wide strips across width of fabric.

BINDING FABRIC

· Cut into six 2½in wide strips across width of fabric.

 Tip

You really have very little wastage from a jelly roll, so don't be too zealous when trimming selvedges.

LIGHT JELLY ROLL STRIPS

· Cut the following rectangles (logs) from the eighteen light jelly roll strips, cutting the longest first:

  - Twelve 2½in x 12½in

  - Twenty 2½in x 10½in

  - Sixteen 2½in x 8½in

  - Sixteen 2½in x 6½in

  - Sixteen 2½in x 4½in

  - Sixteen 2½in x 2½in

DARK JELLY ROLL STRIPS

· Cut the following rectangles (logs) from the twenty-two dark jelly roll strips, cutting the longest first:

  - Sixteen 2½in x 12½in

  - Thirty-two 2½in x 10½in

  - Sixteen 2½in x 8½in

  - Sixteen 2½in x 6½in

  - Sixteen 2½in x 4½in

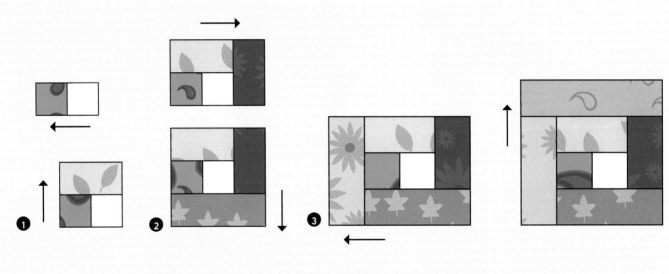

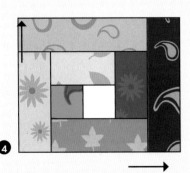

 Tip

Keep your sewing at a constant speed. Chain piecing is a great way to speed up piecing but sewing too fast can produce uneven stitches so a steady pace is preferable and will produce much neater work.

MAKING THE BLOCKS

1. Take a light square and a centre square (shown here as white) and with right sides together, sew together. Press away from centre. Sew a light 2½in x 4½in log to this unit. Press to outer log in direction of arrow (see **diagram 1**).

2. Sew a dark 2½in x 4½in log and press to outer log. Sew a dark 2½in x 6½in log and press to outer log (see **diagram 2**).

3. Sew a light 2½in x 6½in log and press to outer log. Sew a light 2½in x 8½in log and press to outer log (see **diagram 3**).

4. Sew a dark 2½in x 8½in log and press to outer log. Sew a dark 2½in x 10½in log and press to outer log (see **diagram 4**).

5. All the blocks up to this point are the same and chain piecing will speed up the construction. When chain piecing, cut the threads and press before adding the next round of logs. Make sixteen blocks.

6. The last round of logs varies and you need four different kinds of blocks to create the hidden stars, which are numbered to make the layout easier (see **diagram 5**).

CORNER BLOCKS 1, 4, 13, 16

7. Add a 10½in light log and a 12½in light log as before and press seams as indicated by arrows in **diagram 6**.

8. The next 12½in dark log (seen on right-hand side in **diagram 6**) requires a star point. Lay a star square right sides together on the dark log and sew across the diagonal. Flip the square over. Press towards the star fabric and trim the excess. Make sure you have placed the star point in the correct place before cutting the excess (see **diagram 7**).

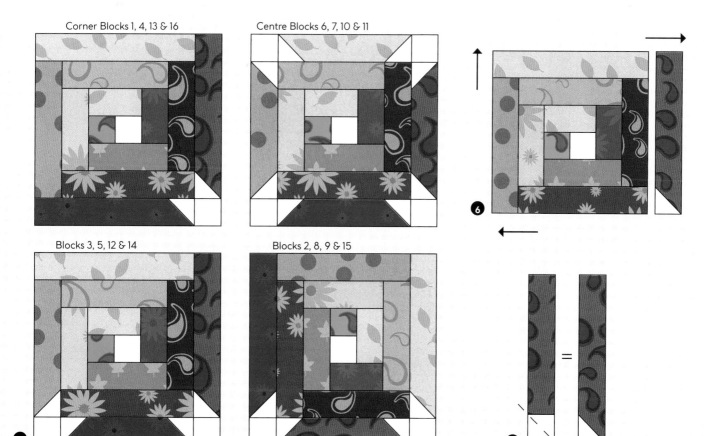

Corner Blocks 1, 4, 13 & 16

Centre Blocks 6, 7, 10 & 11

Blocks 3, 5, 12 & 14

Blocks 2, 8, 9 & 15

9. Sew a star point to the next 12½in log and press open. Sew a star square to one end of it and press, as shown in **diagram 8**.

CENTRE BLOCKS 6, 7, 10, 11

10. Referring to **diagram 9**, add star points and star squares and press as shown. Make four of these blocks.

BLOCKS 3, 5, 12, 14

11. Referring to **diagram 10**, add star points and star squares and press. Make four of these blocks.

BLOCKS 2, 8, 9, 15

12. Referring to **diagram 11**, add star points and star squares and press. Make four of these blocks.

ASSEMBLING THE QUILT

13. Now you have completed 16 blocks you are ready to lay them out, referring to **diagram 12**. Block numbers start at the top left and go across 1 to 4, the second row starts 5 to 8, third row 9 to 12 and the bottom row 13 to 16. When you have made sure they are in the correct place, sew the blocks together, matching seams.

14. Join your six 2½in wide border strips into one continuous length and, referring to Techniques: Adding Borders, add borders to the quilt.

FINISHING THE QUILT

15. Your quilt top is now complete. Quilt as desired and bind to finish (see Techniques: Quilting and Binding a Quilt).

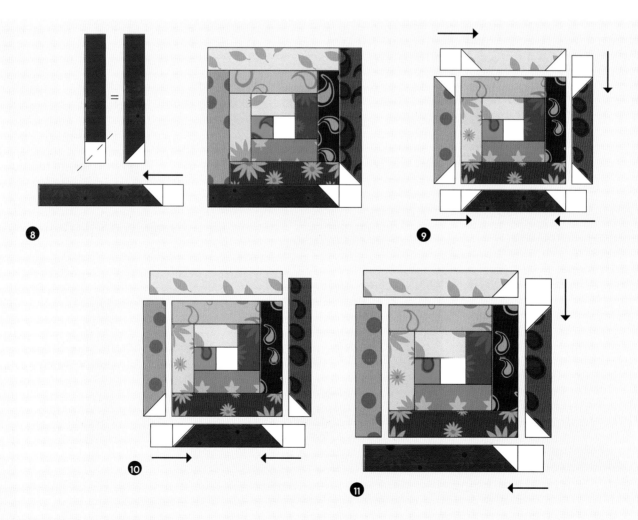

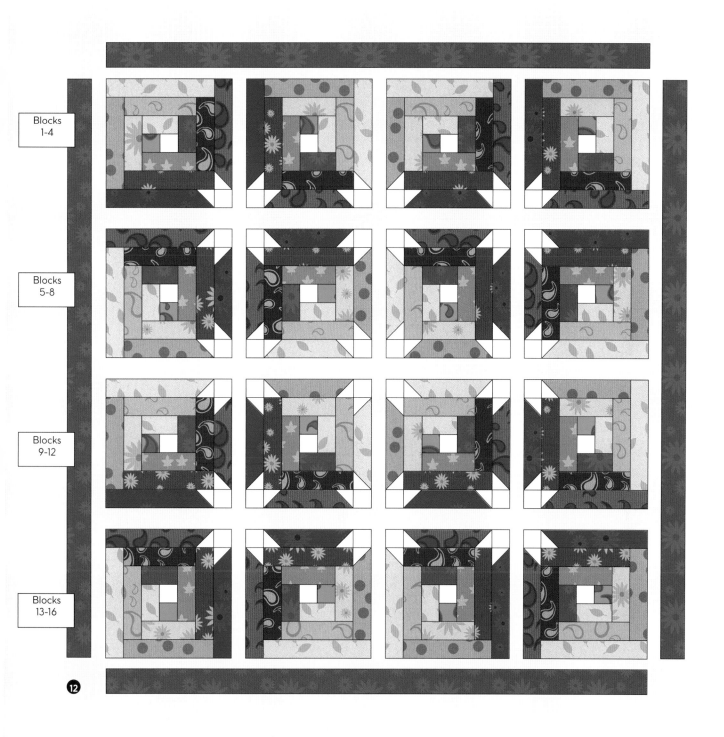

Blocks 1-4

Blocks 5-8

Blocks 9-12

Blocks 13-16

12

 Tip

When butting seams together in machine piecing, try to have the top seam facing the foot of your machine and the bottom seam facing you.

French Lace

Who could resist this lovely jelly roll from French General for Moda? It was just made for this design. You do have to add one strip to your jelly roll but we're sure you have something tucked away in your stash! We hadn't planned at first to add the pieced border but after playing around with the quilt for a while it just materialized. Then we decided it needed an outer border so the quilt kept getting bigger! We hope you like the effect.

VITAL STATISTICS

Quilt size: 72in x 72in
Block size: large 8in, small 4in
Number of blocks: 36 large for centre, 60 small for border
Setting: 6 x 6 blocks for centre, plus 4in unpieced outer border, 4in bow tie block border and 4in unpieced inner border

REQUIREMENTS

- One jelly roll OR forty 2½in strips cut across the width of the fabric
- One 2½in x 42in coordinating strip to add to the jelly roll
- 4yd (3.75m) background fabric
- 24in (60cm) binding fabric

The French Lace quilt showcases two classic blocks that we know and love, that is the snowball and the bow tie. The quilt was pieced by the authors and longarm quilted by The Quilt Room.

CUTTING INSTRUCTIONS

JELLY ROLL STRIPS

- Cut each of the forty jelly roll strips and the one extra 2½in strip as follows, keeping the squares from each fabric together in separate piles:

  - Ten 2½in squares

  - Trim the balance of each strip to measure 1½in wide and then sub-cut each strip into ten 1½in squares

BACKGROUND FABRIC

- Cut twenty-six 2½in wide strips across the width of the fabric and sub-cut each strip into sixteen 2½in squares. You need 408 2½in squares in total.

- From the balance of the fabric (which needs to measure at least 75in long) cut eight 4½in wide border strips lengthways down the fabric. You need the following lengths for the unpieced borders of the quilt but we suggest trimming them to size later once you have checked your own measurements.

  - Two 4½in x 48½in

  - Two 4½in x 56½in

  - Two 4½in x 64½in

  - Two 4½in x 72½in

BINDING FABRIC

- Cut eight 2½in wide strips across the width of the fabric.

MAKING THE SNOWBALL UNITS

1. Working with one pile of fabrics at a time, mark a diagonal line from corner to corner on the wrong side of a 1½in square (see **diagram 1**). This can also be done with a fold, which is our preferred method.

2. With right sides together, lay a marked square on one corner of a 2½in background square, aligning the outer edges as shown in **diagram 2**. Sew across the diagonal, using the marked diagonal line as the stitching line.

3. Flip the jelly roll square over and press towards the outside of the block (see **diagram 3**). Trim the excess fabric from the jelly roll square but do not trim the background fabric. Although this creates a little more bulk, the background fabric helps keep your patchwork in shape. Repeat to make ten of these snowball units.

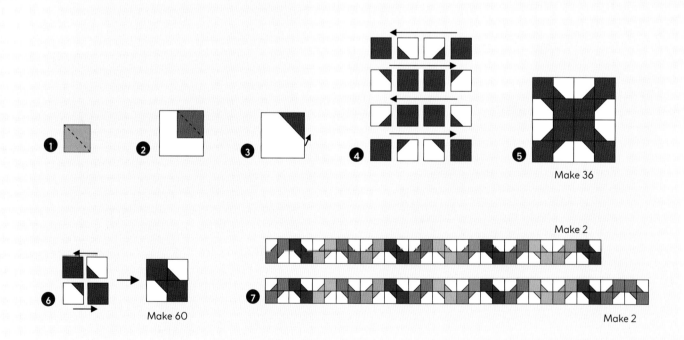

Make 36

Make 60

Make 2

Make 2

4. Take eight snowball units and eight 2½in jelly roll squares and sew together into the large bow tie block as shown in **diagram 4**, pinning at seam intersections to ensure a perfect match. Press alternate rows in opposite directions.

5. Set aside the remaining two snowball units and two 2½in squares from the pile. These will be used later to make the pieced border.

6. Repeat the block-making process to make a total of thirty-six blocks (see **diagram 5**). The remaining five piles of fabric plus the squares set aside are used to make the pieced border.

MAKING THE PIECED BORDER

7. Sew together two 2½in squares and two snowball units from the same fabric as shown in **diagram 6**. Press the work. Repeat to make sixty small bow tie blocks like this.

8. For the side borders, sew fourteen small bow tie blocks together into a row, rotating the blocks to make the pattern shown in **diagram 7**. Repeat to make a second row. Press the work. For the top and bottom borders, sew sixteen bow tie blocks together into a row, as shown. Repeat to make a second row. Press the work.

ASSEMBLING THE QUILT CENTRE

9. Lay out the thirty-six large blocks into six rows of six blocks. When you are happy with the layout, sew the blocks into rows, pinning at all seam intersections. Press alternate rows in opposite directions. Sew the rows together, pinning at all seam intersections to ensure a perfect match, then press (see **diagram 8**).

ADDING THE BORDERS

10. Sew the two 4½in x 48½in unpieced border strips to the side of the quilt, pinning and easing where necessary. Press the work. Now sew the two 4½in x 56½in unpieced border strips to the top and bottom of the quilt and press (see **diagram 9**).

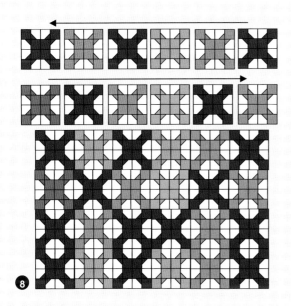

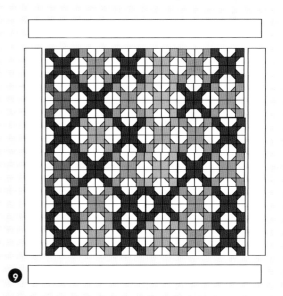

11. Sew the pieced border strips with fourteen bow tie blocks to the sides of the quilt, pinning and easing where necessary, and then press. Sew the pieced border strips with sixteen blocks to the top and bottom of the quilt and press (see **diagram 10**).

12. Sew the two 4½in x 64½in unpieced border strips to the sides of the quilt, pinning and easing where necessary. Press the work. Now sew the two 4½in x 72½in border strips to the top and bottom of the quilt and press well (see **diagram 11**).

FINISHING THE QUILT

13. Your quilt top is now complete. Quilt as desired and bind to finish (see Techniques: Quilting and Binding a Quilt).

10

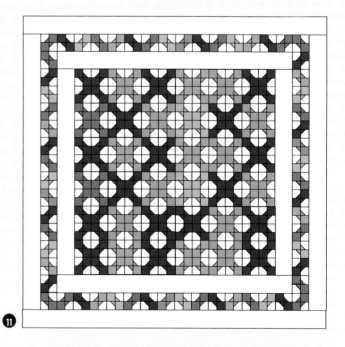

11

Chain Reaction

An antique quilt was our inspiration here but for our modern heirloom we decided that while honouring the design layout of the original quilt we would choose a totally different colour plan. We wanted to use the vibrant colours and extrovert patterns of designer Kaffe Fassett and these fabrics just called out for a dark background to emphasize them. The result is a bold and striking creation that would work well with many contemporary interiors.

VITAL STATISTICS

Quilt size: 76in x 76in
Block size: 12in
Number of blocks: 36
Setting: 6 x 6 blocks, plus 2in border

REQUIREMENTS

- One jelly roll OR forty 2½in strips cut across the width of the fabric

- 2¾yd (2.5m) fabric for the background and border

- 1½yd (1.4m) accent fabric

- 24in (60cm) binding fabric

The quilt went together very easily and was quick and simple to sew together thanks to some clever strip piecing. The quilt was pieced by the authors and longarm quilted by The Quilt Room.

CUTTING INSTRUCTIONS

JELLY ROLL STRIPS

· Cut all forty jelly roll strips in half to create eighty rectangles measuring 2½in x 22in approximately.

ACCENT FABRIC

· Cut twenty 2½in strips across the width of the fabric and cut each in half to create forty rectangles approximately 2½in x 22in.

BACKGROUND FABRIC

· Cut thirteen strips 2½in wide across the fabric width. Set eight aside for the borders.

· Cut the remaining five 2½in wide strips in half to create ten rectangles approximately 2½in x 22in.

· Cut five 4½in strips across the width of the fabric and cut each in half to create ten rectangles approximately 4½in x 22in.

· Cut five 6½in wide strips across the fabric width and cut each in half to create ten rectangles approximately 6½in x 22in.

BINDING FABRIC

· Cut eight 2½in wide strips across the width of the fabric.

SORTING THE CUT FABRIC STRIPS

After cutting your fabrics, make five separate piles as follows:

· Eighty jelly roll rectangles.

· Forty accent rectangles.

· Ten 2½in wide background rectangles.

· Ten 4½in background rectangles.

· Ten 6½in background rectangles.

MAKING THE STRIP UNITS

1. You now need to make three different strip units – Unit A, Unit B and Unit C.

STRIP UNIT A

2. Choose three jelly roll rectangles, two accent rectangles and one 2½in background rectangle and sew them into strip Unit A (see **diagram 1, Unit A**). Don't spend too much time on your selection; use what's next in the pile unless it's too similar. Press the seams as shown. Repeat to make ten strip Unit As.

3. Lay one strip Unit A on the cutting mat at a time. Trim the selvedge and sub-cut into eight 2½in segments (see **diagram 2**). Always line up the markings on the ruler with the seams to make sure you are cutting at a right angle. Cut eighty Unit A segments.

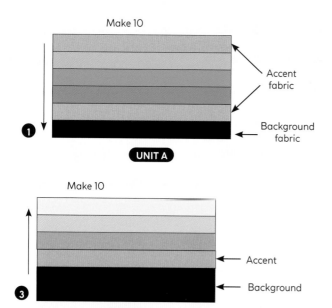

Make 10

Accent fabric

Background fabric

❶

UNIT A

Make 10

Accent

Background

❸

UNIT B

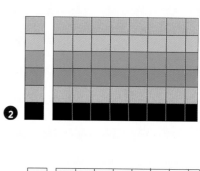

❷

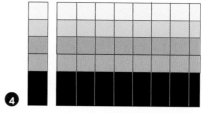

❹

STRIP UNIT B

4. Choose three jelly roll rectangles, one accent rectangle and one 4½in background rectangle and sew them into strip Unit B. Press seams as shown in **diagram 3, Unit B**. Repeat to make ten strip Unit Bs.

5. Lay one strip Unit B on the cutting mat at a time. Trim the selvedge and sub-cut into eight 2½in wide segments in the same way as you did for strip Unit A (see **diagram 4**). Cut eighty Unit B segments.

STRIP UNIT C

6. Choose two jelly roll rectangles, one accent rectangle and one 6½in background rectangle and sew them into strip Unit C. Press seams as shown in **diagram 5, Unit C**. Repeat to make ten strip Unit Cs.

7. Lay one strip Unit C on the cutting mat at a time. Trim the selvedge and sub-cut into eight 2½in segments (see **diagram 6**), just as you did for strip Units A and B. Cut eighty Unit C segments.

8. Put the Unit A, Unit B and Unit C segments into three piles (see **diagram 7**), making sure that the background fabric always faces the same way.

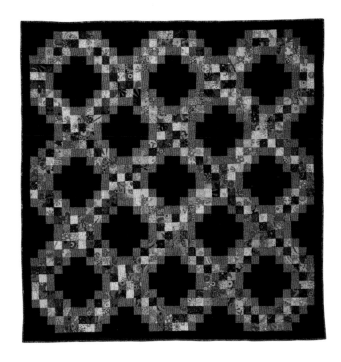

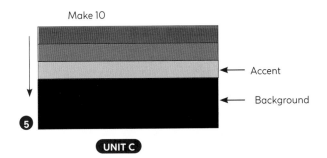

Make 10

Accent

Background

5

UNIT C

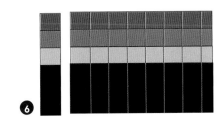

6

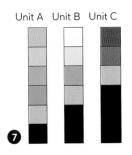

Unit A　Unit B　Unit C

7

MAKING THE BLOCKS

9. Choose one Unit A, one Unit B and one Unit C and sew together as shown in **diagram 8**, pinning at every seam intersection to ensure a perfect match. The seams will nest together nicely. Try to have different fabrics next to each other. Repeat to make eighty units like this. Press seams towards Unit C as shown. Seventy-two units are needed for the quilt. The extra eight units will make four blocks, which could be used to create a coordinating cushion.

10. Choose two of these units and rotate one of the units 180 degrees as shown in **diagram 9**. Sew together, pinning at every seam intersection to ensure a perfect match and then press. Repeat to make thirty-six blocks for the quilt. You could make up the extra four blocks at this stage if you like.

ASSEMBLING THE QUILT

11. Referring to **diagram 10**, lay out the blocks into six rows of six blocks each, rotating alternate blocks 90 degrees. When you are happy with the layout, sew the blocks into rows and then sew the rows together, pinning at every seam intersection to ensure a perfect match

12. Join the border strips into a continuous length. Determine the vertical measurement from top to bottom through the centre of your quilt top. Cut two side borders to this measurement. Pin and sew to the quilt and press.

13. Now determine the horizontal measurement from side to side across the centre of the quilt top. Cut two borders to this measurement. Sew to the top and bottom of your quilt and press (see **diagram 11**).

FINISHING THE QUILT

14. Your quilt top is complete. Quilt as desired and bind to finish (see Techniques: Quilting and Binding a Quilt).

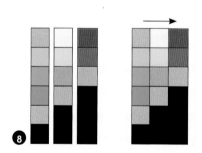

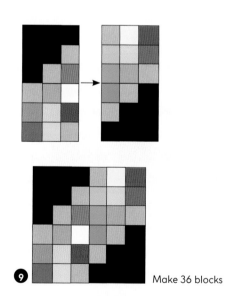

Make 36 blocks

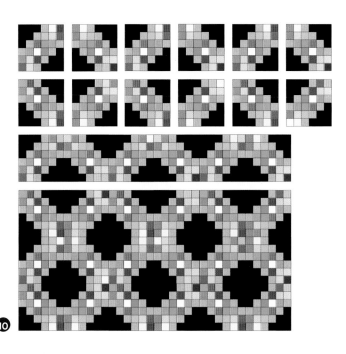

10

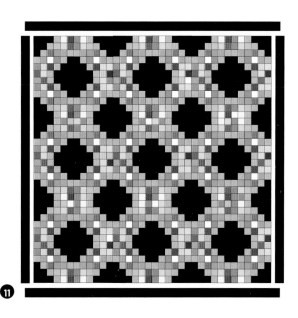

11

Honeycomb

Hexagons are always fun and the strippy ones in this quilt are quick to make as they are pieced half-hexagons sewn together, with no set-in seams needed. You need to use a jelly roll that has a range of colours, as the design would be lost if you had hexagons of similar colours next to each other. We used a lovely jelly roll from Blackbird Designs called Wild Orchid. We loved the range of pinks, lilacs and yellows going deeper into browns and blacks. It was the perfect choice for this quilt. We edged it with a solid taupe border, which sets the fabrics off nicely.

VITAL STATISTICS

Quilt size: 55in x 65in
Setting: Seven vertical rows, plus 4½in border

REQUIREMENTS

· One jelly roll OR forty 2½in strips cut across the width of the fabric

· 1½yd (1.4m) border fabric

· 20in (50cm) binding fabric

· 60-degree triangle measuring at least 8in

One would normally expect to hand-piece hexagons over papers so what a treat to be able to make these strippy hexagons quickly and easily on the machine. The quilt was pieced by the authors and longarm quilted by The Quilt Room.

SORTING THE STRIPS

Pair up the forty strips into twenty pairs. Try to have each fabric in a pair in a similar colour, although if you have duplicates in your jelly roll avoid using them together as you will lose the strippy effect.

CUTTING INSTRUCTIONS

BORDER FABRIC

· Cut seven 4½in wide strips across the width of the fabric (for half-hexagons).

· Cut three 5in wide strips across the width of the fabric (for top and bottom borders).

BINDING FABRIC

· Cut six 2½in wide strips across the width of the fabric.

STRIP PIECING THE HEXAGONS

1. Sew your pairs of jelly roll strips into twenty strip units. Press in the direction shown in **diagram 1**.

2. Take one of these strip units and place the 60-degree triangle on the strip as shown in **diagram 2**, with the 3½in line of the ruler along the top and the 8in line along the bottom. Mark these lines on the triangle with masking tape to make sure you always line up on the correct markings. Cut the first half-hexagon.

3. Rotate the triangle 180 degrees (see **diagram 3**) and continue in this way to cut five half-hexagons from one strip unit (see Tip).

4. Repeat with all twenty strip units to cut at least 100 jelly roll half-hexagons (see **diagram 4**). Keep the half-hexagons from each strip unit together.

5. Take a 4½in border strip and using the same marked triangle, cut five border half-hexagons from one strip, rotating the ruler 180 degrees alternately along the strip (see **diagram 5**).

6. Repeat with all seven 4½in border strips to make a total of thirty-five border half-hexagons (see **diagram 6**). You need thirty-four, so one will be spare.

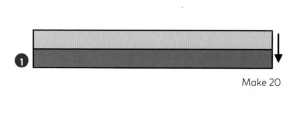

Make 20

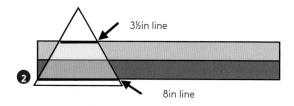

3½in line

8in line

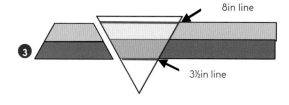

8in line

3½in line

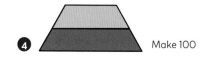

Make 100

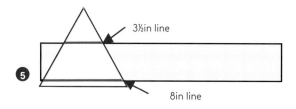

3½in line

8in line

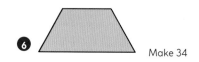

Make 34

ASSEMBLING THE QUILT

7. Lay out the pieced half-hexagons to form full hexagons as shown in **diagram 7**, trying not to have similar colours next to each other. Place the border half-hexagons at the end of each row and insert as shown in the top and bottom rows. You will have some half-hexagons spare.

8. When you are happy with the layout, sew the half-hexagons into rows. When joining strips with angled cuts there will be an overlap at each end, as shown in **diagram 8**, so check for accuracy.

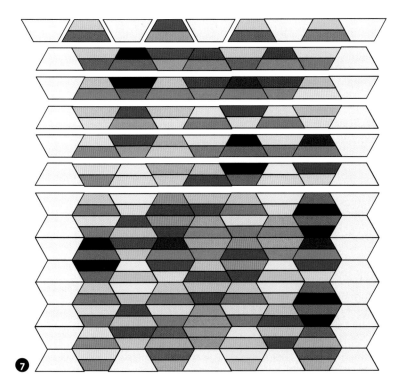

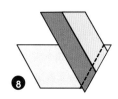

▶▶▶ *Tip*

We managed to cut six half-hexagons from some of our longer strips and although you do not need extra, it does give you a little more choice when laying out the hexagons prior to sewing.

9. When you have finished the first row, press the seams in one direction (see **diagram 9**). Continue sewing rows, pressing the seams of alternate rows in opposite directions so that when sewing the rows together the seams will nest together nicely.

10. Sew the rows together, pinning at all seam intersections to ensure a perfect match, and then press (see **diagram 10**).

11. Using a long quilting ruler, straighten the uneven side edges of the quilt (see **diagram 11**).

ADDING THE TOP AND BOTTOM BORDERS

12. Sew the three 5in wide border strips into a continuous length. Determine the horizontal measurement of the quilt and cut two borders to this length. Pin and sew to the top and bottom of the quilt and press (see **diagram 12**).

FINISHING THE QUILT

13. Your quilt top is complete. Quilt as desired and bind to finish (see Techniques: Quilting and Binding a Quilt).

 Tip

Do label your quilts on the back to let the next generation know who made the quilt plus any other interesting details you want to add. We love discovering quilt labels on antique quilts. Don't forget to take photos!

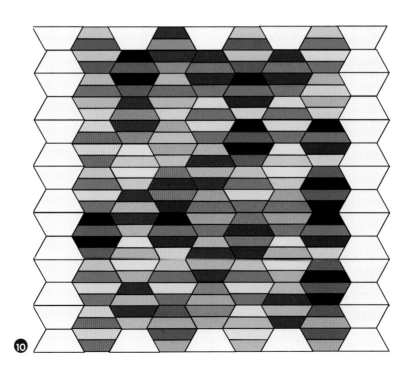

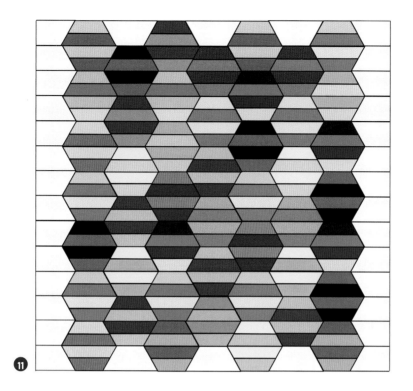

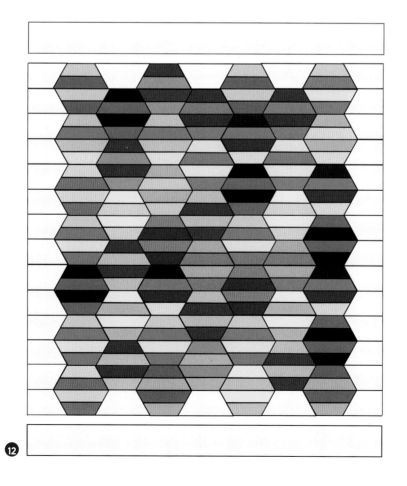

Nine-Patch Sunburst

If you are keen enough to want to make lots of nine-patch blocks and then cut them in half then this is the quilt for you! It's actually a fun quilt to make and the piecing can be achieved in a weekend thanks to a strip piecing technique for creating the nine-patch units. It makes a good size quilt with an eye-catching pattern that radiates outwards from the quilt centre. We chose a pastel Kaffe Fassett strip roll and used a Kaffe Fassett pale lilac spot that we really loved for the background, which makes the colours sing.

VITAL STATISTICS

Quilt size: 66in x 66in
Block size: 5½in
Number of blocks: 144
Setting: 12 x 12 blocks

REQUIREMENTS

- One jelly roll OR forty 2½in strips cut across the width of the fabric
- 2¾yd (2.5m) background fabric
- 20in (50cm) binding fabric

The fabrics in this quilt really 'zing' and we chose a quilting design with a clamshell pattern, which was just perfect. The quilt was pieced by the authors and longarm quilted by The Quilt Room.

SORTING THE STRIPS

There is no sorting of strips necessary as this is a very scrappy quilt. You will only need thirty-six strips. Four strips are spare.

CUTTING INSTRUCTIONS

BACKGROUND FABRIC

· Cut eleven 6½in wide strips across the width of the fabric and sub-cut each strip into six 6½in squares to make a total of sixty-six 6½in squares. You need sixty-two (four are spare).

· Cut three 6in wide strips across the width of the fabric and sub-cut each strip into seven 6in squares to make a total of twenty-one 6in squares. You need twenty (one is spare).

BINDING FABRIC

· Cut seven 2½in wide strips across the width of the fabric.

MAKING THE NINE-PATCH UNITS

1. Choose three jelly roll strips and sew them together down the long sides to form a strip unit, as shown in **diagram 1**. Sew one strip in one direction and one in the other direction and this will prevent the strip units bowing. Press the sewn strips in one direction, as shown. Repeat with the remaining jelly roll strips to make twelve strip units in total.

2. Take each strip unit, trim the selvedge and then cut the strip unit into sixteen 2½in segments (see **diagram 2**).

3. Repeat with all twelve strip units to make a total of 192 segments each 2½in wide (see **diagram 3**). You need 186, so six are spare.

4. Choose two segments and sew together as shown in **diagram 4**. You may need to rotate one segment so the seams nest together nicely. Pin at the seam intersections to ensure a perfect match, although you may find that once the seams are nested together nicely it is not necessary to pin.

5. Choose a third segment and sew together as shown in **diagram 5**, rotating the segment so that the seams nest together. Press the seams. The sewn nine-patch unit should be 6½in square.

6. Repeat this process to make sixty-two nine-patch units in total. Chain piecing will speed up this process.

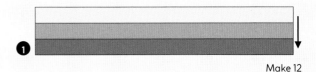

Make 12

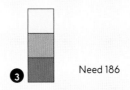

Need 186

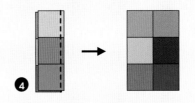

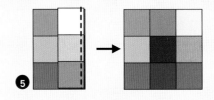

Make 62 nine-patch units

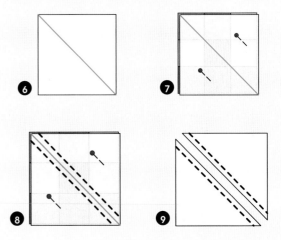

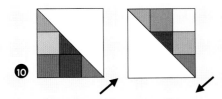

 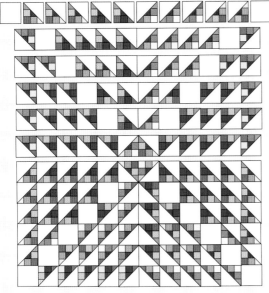

ASSEMBLING THE BLOCKS

7. Take the sixty-two 6½in background squares and draw a diagonal line on the reverse side as shown in **diagram 6**.

8. Lay one marked background square on top of one nine-patch unit, right sides together and aligning the edges. Pin in position (see **diagram 7**).

9. Stitch along both sides of the drawn line with a scant ¼in seam allowance (see **diagram 8**).

10. Press the stitches to set them and then cut along the drawn diagonal line (see **diagram 9**). Trim off dog ears.

11. Open the blocks and press towards the background fabric (see **diagram 10**). Check the block is 6in square at this stage. Repeat with all sixty-two nine-patch units to make 124 blocks in total.

ASSEMBLING THE QUILT

12. Lay out the pieced blocks and the 6in background squares in twelve rows each with twelve blocks, referring often to **diagram 11**. Take great care: it is easy to rotate a block wrongly and spoil the sunburst pattern.

13. When you are happy with the layout, sew the blocks into rows and then sew the rows together, pinning at all seam intersections to ensure a perfect match (see **diagram 12**).

FINISHING THE QUILT

14. Your quilt top is complete. Quilt as desired and bind to finish (see Techniques: Quilting and Binding a Quilt).

Kaleidoscope

VITAL STATISTICS

Quilt size: 34in x 44in
Block size: 10in
Number of blocks: 12
Setting: 3 x 4 blocks, plus 2in border

Our Kaleidoscope quilt and the Jigsaw quilt (see Jigsaw) were both made from just one jelly roll! We used a French General Rural Jardin jelly roll as we loved the combination of dark blues and reds coupled with gentler colours. For Kaleidoscope we pulled out the dark reds and dark blues to create a dynamic looking quilt. We didn't have many true neutrals in the range so we chose the pale blue as our neutral. Be guided by what is in your jelly roll — the fabrics all blend together beautifully which should give you confidence.

REQUIREMENTS

- Half a jelly roll OR twenty 2½in strips cut across the width of the fabric

- 12in (30cm) fabric to match colour A (dark red)

- 12in (30cm) fabric for centre squares

- 12in (30cm) border fabric

- 12in (30cm) binding fabric

- Creative Grids 45/90 ruler or other speciality ruler

This is a great quilt — so dynamic and interesting with the focus on those lovely dark reds and dark blues. It's easy to piece too. The quilt was pieced by the authors and longarm quilted by The Quilt Room.

SORTING THE STRIPS

- Choose five strips for colour A (dark red).
- Choose four strips for colour B (blue).
- Choose two strips for colour C (aqua).
- Choose two strips for colour D (light red).
- Choose six neutral strips.
- One strip is spare.

CUTTING INSTRUCTIONS

JELLY ROLL STRIPS

- Take three of the colour A (dark red) strips and cut each into sixteen squares 2½in x 2½in. You need forty-eight in total. Leave the remaining two dark red strips uncut.
- Take two colour B (blue) strips and trim them to measure 1½in x 42in. Sub-cut each strip into twenty-four squares 1½in x 1½in. You need forty-eight in total. Leave the remaining two blue strips uncut.
- Take the two colour D (light red) strips and cut each into twelve squares 2½in x 2½in. You need twenty-four in total.
- Take four of the neutral strips and cut each into six rectangles 2½in x 6½in. You need twenty-four in total. Leave the remaining two neutral strips uncut.

EXTRA FABRIC – COLOUR A (DARK RED)

- Cut six strips 1½in wide across the width of the fabric.
- Sub-cut each strip into eight rectangles 1½in x 4½in. You need forty-eight in total.

EXTRA FABRIC – CENTRE SQUARES

- Cut two strips 4½in wide across the width of the fabric.
- Sub-cut each strip into six squares 4½in x 4½in. You need twelve in total.

BORDER FABRIC

- Cut four 2½in wide strips across the width of the fabric.

BINDING FABRIC

- Cut four 2½in wide strips across the width of the fabric.

MAKING THE HALF-SQUARE TRIANGLE UNITS

1. Take two colour C (aqua) jelly roll strips and two colour B (blue) jelly roll strips. Press one aqua and one blue strip right sides together ensuring that they are exactly one on top of the other (see **diagram 1**). The pressing will help to hold the two strips together.

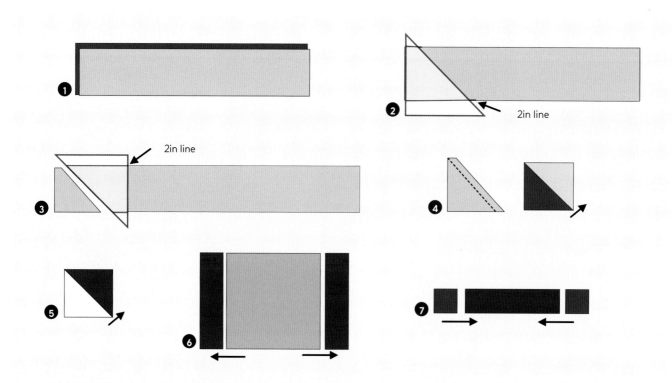

2. Lay out on a cutting mat and trim the selvedge on the left side. Position your ruler, lining up the 2in mark at the bottom edge of the strips, and cut the first triangle (see **diagram 2**). You will notice that the cut-out triangle has a flat top. This would just have been a dog ear you needed to cut off – so it is saving you time!

3. Rotate the ruler 180 degrees to the right as shown in **diagram 3** and cut the next triangle. Continue along the strip. You need twenty-four sets of triangles from one strip.

4. Sew along the diagonals to form twenty-four half-square triangles, chain piecing for speed. Trim all dog ears and then press open with the seams pressed towards the aqua (lighter) fabric (see **diagram 4**). Repeat with the other aqua and blue strips to make forty-eight aqua and blue half-square triangles in total.

5. Take two colour A (dark red) and two neutral jelly roll strips and repeat steps 1–4 to make forty-eight dark red and neutral half-square triangle units (see **diagram 5**). Press towards the darker fabric.

MAKING THE CENTRES OF BLOCKS A & B

6. Take two dark red 1½in x 4½in rectangles and sew to either side of a 4½in centre square (see **diagram 6**). Press as shown. Repeat to create twelve of these units.

7. Take two colour B (blue) 1½in squares and sew to either side of a colour A (dark red) 1½in x 4½in rectangle (see **diagram 7**). Press as shown. Repeat to create twenty-four of these units.

8. Sew these units to the top and bottom, pinning at every seam intersection to ensure a perfect match. Press as shown in **diagram 8**. Repeat to make twelve centre units.

MAKING BLOCK A

9. Sew two dark red and neutral half-square triangle units to either side of a light red square as shown in **diagram 9**. Press the work. Repeat to make four of these units.

10. Sew two of these units to either side of a centre square as shown in **diagram 10** and then press the work.

11. Sew two aqua and blue half-square triangle units to either side of the other two units (see **diagram 11**). Press the work.

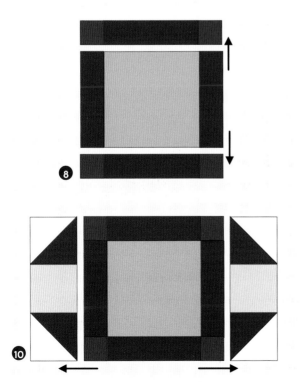

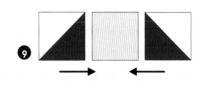

12. Sew these to the top and bottom to create Block A, pinning at every seam intersection to ensure a perfect match (see **diagram 12, Block A**). Repeat to make six of Block A.

MAKING BLOCK B

13. Take one dark red 2½in square and lay it right sides together on a 2½in x 6½in neutral rectangle as shown in **diagram 13** and sew across the diagonal. Folding your square to mark the diagonal line will help keep your stitching accurate.

14. Flip the square over and press towards the dark red fabric as shown in **diagram 14**. Trim the excess dark red fabric but do not trim the neutral fabric. Although this creates a little more bulk, this neutral rectangle keeps your units in shape.

15. Place a second dark red 2½in square and lay it on the other side as shown and sew across the diagonal. Flip the square over and press the work (see **diagram 15**). Trim the excess dark red fabric. Repeat to make four units.

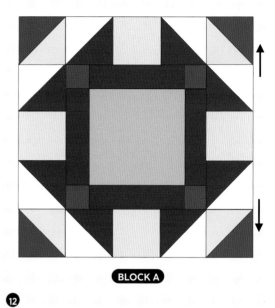

BLOCK A

12

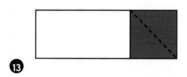

13

14

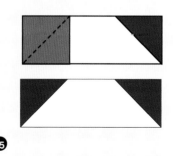

15

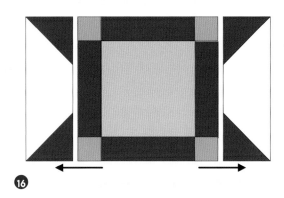

16.

16. Sew two of these units to either side of a centre square and press as shown in **diagram 16**.

17. Sew two aqua and blue half-square triangle units to either side of the other two units and press as shown in **diagram 17**.

18. Now sew these units to the top and bottom to create Block B (see **diagram 18, Block B**), pinning at every seam intersection to ensure a perfect match. Press the work. Repeat this process to make six of Block B.

17.

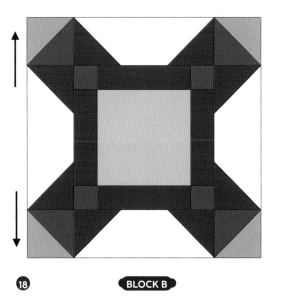

18. **BLOCK B**

ASSEMBLING THE QUILT

19. Referring to **diagram 19**, lay out the blocks into rows, alternating Block A and Block B. Make four rows of three blocks as shown.

20. When you are happy with the layout, sew the blocks into rows, pressing the rows in alternate directions as shown. Then sew the rows together, pinning at every seam intersection to ensure that you have matching seams. Press the work.

ADDING THE BORDERS

21. Referring to **diagram 20** and Techniques: Adding Borders, add the borders to the quilt. Add the side borders first and you won't need to join the border strips into a continuous length.

FINISHING THE QUILT

22. Your quilt top is complete. Quilt as desired and bind to finish (see Techniques: Quilting and Binding a Quilt).

20

Jigsaw

The Jigsaw quilt is made from the very same jelly roll as the Kaleidoscope quilt (see Kaleidoscope). This little quilt ended up being one of our all-time favourites. The gentler colours from the jelly roll worked so well together and created a deliciously calm quilt. What is there not to like about this quilt!

VITAL STATISTICS

Quilt size: 36in x 42in
Block size: 6in
Number of blocks: 30
Setting: 5 x 6 blocks, plus 2in sawtooth top and left border and 2in outer border

REQUIREMENTS

- Half a jelly roll OR twenty 2½in strips cut across the width of the fabric
- 1¼yd (1.1m) background fabric
- 16in (40cm) binding fabric
- Creative Grids 45/90 ruler or other speciality ruler

What a gorgeous quilt this is. It took us a while to fathom out how to create this design using jelly roll strips but it turned out to be very simple – it always is once you know how! The quilt was pieced by the authors and longarm quilted by The Quilt Room.

SORTING THE STRIPS

- Choose sixteen strips and make up eight pairs of strips in similar colours.

- Choose one strip to be added to the outer border.

- Three strips are spare.

CUTTING INSTRUCTIONS

JELLY ROLL STRIPS

- Take the sixteen jelly roll strips which are now in pairs and cut into the following rectangles, keeping the 12in and 21in rectangles from the pairs together:

  - 2½in x 12in rectangle

  - 2½in x 21in rectangle

  - 2½in x 9in rectangle and set these aside for the outer border

- Take the other strip and cut into four rectangles 2½in x 9in and set aside with the others already cut for the outer border.

BACKGROUND FABRIC

- Cut three 4½in wide strips across the width of the fabric.

- Sub-cut each strip into three rectangles 4½in x 12in. You need eight in total (one is spare.)

- Cut eight 2½in wide strips across the width of the fabric and cut each in half to create two rectangles 2½in x 21in. You need sixteen in total.

BINDING FABRIC

- Cut four 2½in wide strips across the width of the fabric.

MAKING THE BLOCKS

1. Working with one pair of jelly roll strips, take a pair of 2½in x 12in rectangles and, with right sides together, sew down the long side. Open and press the work (see **diagram 1**).

2. With right sides together, lay this unit on a 4½in x 12in background strip aligning the edges and press to hold in place. It is important to always have the background strip on the bottom. Trim the left-hand selvedge. Position the ruler, lining up the 4in mark at the bottom edge of the strips, and cut the first triangle (see **diagram 2**). You will notice that the cut-out triangle has a flat top. This would just have been a dog ear you needed to cut off — so it is saving you time!

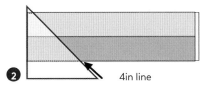

4in line

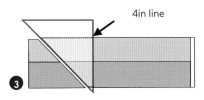

4in line

x 2   x 2

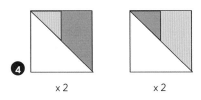

2in line

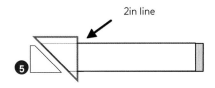

x 12   x 12

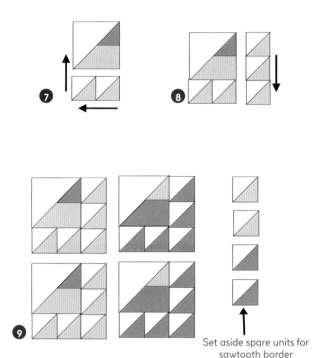

Set aside spare units for sawtooth border

3. Rotate the ruler 180 degrees to the right as shown in **diagram 3** and cut the next triangle. Repeat to cut four pairs of triangles.

4. Sew along the diagonals to form four 4in half-square triangle units. Trim all dog ears and press open (see **diagram 4**). You will have two each of two different 4in half-square triangle units.

5. Still working with the same pair of jelly roll strips, take one of the 2½in x 21in jelly roll rectangles and a 2½in x 21in background rectangle and lay them right sides together – it doesn't matter which fabric is on top. Press to hold in place. Using the ruler as before but this time using the 2in line for cutting, cut twelve pairs of triangles as shown in **diagram 5**. Sew along the diagonals to form twelve 2in half-square triangle units and press open.

6. Repeat with the other 2½in x 21in jelly roll strip to make a further twelve 2in half-square triangle units as shown in **diagram 6**. Press open. You now have twenty-four in total.

7. Take five identical 2in half-square triangle units. Sew two together as shown and sew to the bottom of a 4in half-square triangle unit (see **diagram 7**). Press as shown. We chose to have our fabrics match the base of the large triangle but you could have them match the top or mix them all up – the choice is yours.

8. Sew the other three 2in half-square triangle units together as shown in **diagram 8**. Press and sew to the right-hand side, pinning at the seam intersections to ensure a perfect match.

9. Repeat steps 1–8 to make four blocks as shown in **diagram 9**. Set aside the extra four 2in half-square triangle units for the sawtooth border.

10. Repeat steps 1–9 to use all your eight pairs of jelly roll strips. You only need thirty blocks so when working with the final pair of strips, piece only two blocks. Leave the remaining two blocks unpieced, as two of the 2in half-square triangle units are needed for the sawtooth border. You need a total of thirty-four 2in half-square triangle units for the sawtooth border.

ASSEMBLING THE QUILT

11. Lay out the blocks into six rows of five blocks. When you are happy with the layout, sew the blocks into rows and then sew the rows together (see **diagram 10**). Pin at every seam intersection to ensure matching seams. Be prepared when sewing the blocks together to re-press the occasional seam to ensure they nest together nicely and create less bulk.

ADDING THE SAWTOOTH BORDER

12. The sawtooth border is only needed on the top and left-hand side of the quilt. Sew eighteen 2in half-square triangles together as shown in **diagram 11**. These are for the left-hand sawtooth border.

13. Sew sixteen 2in half-square triangles together (see **diagram 12**). These are for the top sawtooth border.

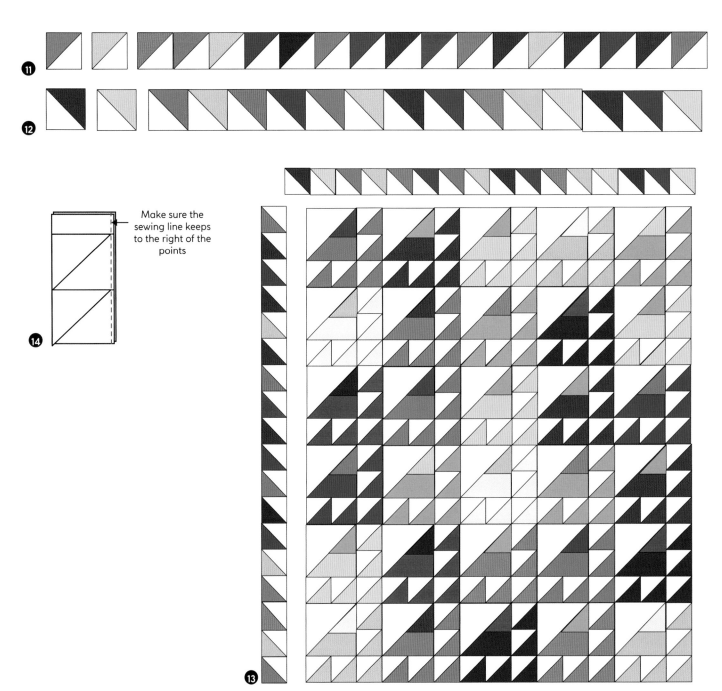

Make sure the sewing line keeps to the right of the points

14. Sew the left-hand side border on first, pinning and easing if necessary and then press the work carefully. Sew on the top border, pinning and easing if necessary (see **diagram 13**). Press the work.

Note: when sewing pieced units together that have points, you don't want to lose those points, so make sure you sew to the *right* of the points and you won't lose the nice sharp tips (see **diagram 14**).

ADDING THE OUTER BORDER

15. Join five 2½in x 9in rectangles into a continuous length and press the work. Repeat to make four of these.

16. Referring to Techniques: Adding Borders, add the outer border to the quilt, adding the side borders first and trimming where required (see **diagram 15**).

17. Your quilt top is complete. Quilt as desired and bind to finish (see Techniques: Quilting and Binding a Quilt).

Neapolitan

This is a classic Trip Around the World design brought up to date with subtle shades of aqua, pink, green and yellow, designed by Tanya Whelan. You need four similar sets of sixteen strips for each of the four quarters of this quilt, otherwise you might lose the distinct design. We used four identical jelly babies (twenty jelly roll strips in each baby), which was absolutely perfect, but two jelly rolls will work. You need to sort them a little more but artistic licence can be used. If you press your seams as we have suggested, there really is no need for pinning, as your seams will butt together nicely.

VITAL STATISTICS

Quilt size: 64in x 64in
Quarter quilt size: 32in x 32in
Number of blocks: 4
Setting: 2 x 2 blocks

REQUIREMENTS

· Two jelly rolls OR four jelly babies OR eighty 2½in strips cut across the width of the fabric

· Spare jelly roll strips for scrappy binding

For those familiar with our patterns, you will know we normally use 'just one jelly roll' for each quilt design. We are ringing the changes with this quilt as one jelly roll wasn't enough! The quilt was pieced by the authors and longarm quilted by The Quilt Room.

SORTING THE STRIPS

· Divide your jelly rolls into four sets of sixteen strips, ensuring each set has similar colours. Each set will make one quarter of your quilt. Using four identical jelly babies is easier as you know you have four strips of each fabric.

· Spend some time deciding in which order to sew your strips together. To assist in your decision, note that strip 1 will be the top left corner fabric – we used aqua. Strip 15 becomes the centre fabric of the quilt, surrounded by strip 14. Strip 16 (orange) is the only fabric that has a full 'round' and has no repeat.

· Reserve seven strips for a scrappy binding.

· Nine strips are spare.

MAKING THE QUARTER-BLOCKS

1. Once you have decided on the order of your strips, sew strips 1 and 2 right sides together down the length. Then sew strip 3 to strip 2, making sure you sew in the opposite direction. This will prevent your strip unit bowing. Continue to add strips until all sixteen strips are sewn together (see **diagram 1**). This will make one quarter of your quilt.

2. Press each seam in the opposite direction to the next seam. This is very important as it will ensure your seams nest together nicely.

3. Once pressed, fold the strip unit right sides together and pin strip 1 to strip 16, lengthways. Sew together to form a tube (see **diagram 2**).

4. Lay the tube flat on your cutting mat, carefully making sure there are no folds anywhere, and then cut the tube into sixteen 2½in segments (see **diagram 3**).

5. Taking one 2½in segment, unpick the seam between strips 1 and 16 (see **diagram 4**).

6. Take the next segment and unpick the seam between strips 1 and 2. Then take the next segment and unpick the seam between 2 and 3. Continue to do this with all sixteen segments, keeping the segments in the correct order, as shown in **diagram 5**.

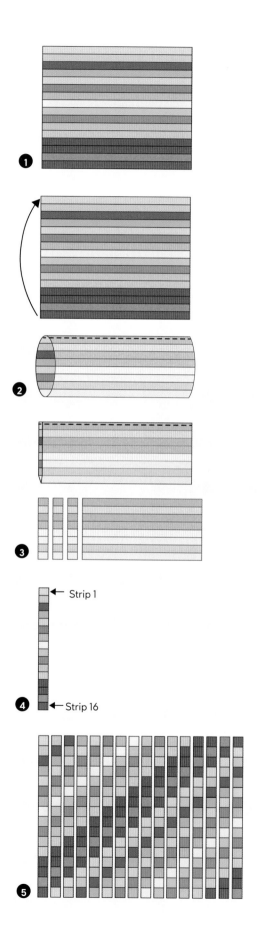

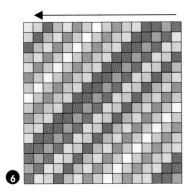

7. Sew the rows together to form a block (which is a quarter of the quilt). As your seams are pressed in alternate directions, they will butt together nicely. You may wish to use a few pins at the seam intersections to start with, but we found after a while that it was unnecessary to pin. Press seams in one direction, as shown in **diagram 6**.

8. Repeat the process to make three more blocks like this.

MAKING THE QUILT

9. Rotate the four blocks so they make the pattern shown in **diagram 7**. Sew the blocks together, ensuring the seams match. You may have to re-press and pin a number of seams so that they butt together nicely. When all seams are sewn, press well.

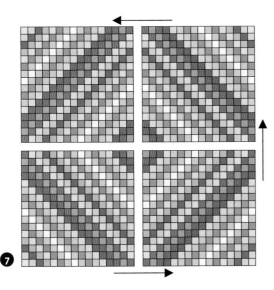

FINISHING THE QUILT

10. Your quilt top is now complete (see **diagram 8**). Quilt as desired and bind to finish (see Techniques: Quilting and Binding a Quilt). To make a scrappy binding, cut each of the seven jelly roll strips allocated for the binding into four pieces. Mix them up and sew them together into a continuous length, making sure you do not sew rectangles of the same fabric next to each other.

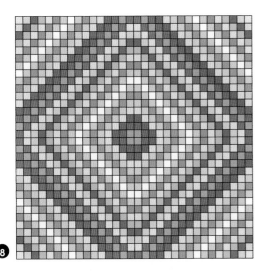

Pandora's Box

The muted, earthy colours of Japanese taupes are subtle and sophisticated and blend together so well. This quilt would particularly complement a room that features natural materials, such as wood and leather. We chose a black print border and quilted dragonflies all over, which added depth and texture.

VITAL STATISTICS

Quilt size: 52in x 76in
Block size: 8in
Number of blocks: 40
Setting: 5 x 8 blocks, plus 6in border

REQUIREMENTS

· One jelly roll OR forty 2½in strips cut across the width of the fabric

· 1¼yd (1.1m) border fabric

· 20in (50cm) binding fabric

We have seen this quilt made up in so many different colourways and they always look stunning. Our choice of a dragonfly quilting design has also been a huge favourite. The quilt was pieced by the authors and quilted by The Quilt Room.

CUTTING INSTRUCTIONS

JELLY ROLL STRIPS

· Trim the selvedge and cut each strip into four rectangles: two of 2½in x 4½in and two of 2½in x 8½in. The remaining 18in or so of each strip is for making your four-patch blocks.

· Stack your cut pieces of strips into four separate piles keeping the fabric in the same order, so that each pile is identical. This is very important if you want to chain piece.

BORDER FABRIC

· Cut six 6½in wide strips across the width of the fabric.

BINDING FABRIC

· Cut seven 2½in wide strips across the width of the fabric.

MAKING THE FOUR-PATCH BLOCKS

1. Using the strips you have saved for your four-patch blocks, sew two contrasting strips together. Press seams to the dark side (see **diagram 1**). Repeat until you have twenty.

2. Cut each one of these joined strips into 2½in segments (see **diagram 2**). You only need four from each joined strip for your quilt, so any extras are spare.

 Tip

*For accuracy, don't stackpile your strips when cutting the segments in **diagram 2**. Check you are cutting perfect rectangles by putting one of your ruler guides on the seam line.*

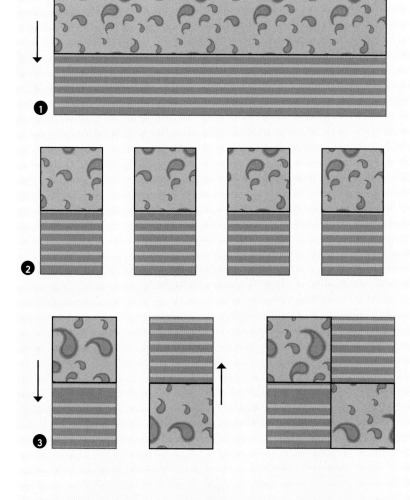

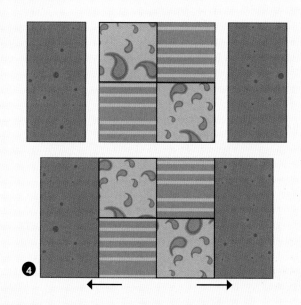

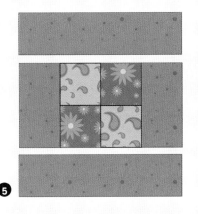

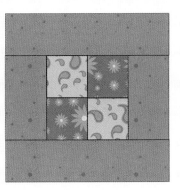

5

6

3. Rotate one segment and, matching the centre seams, sew your four-patch block, as shown in **diagram 3**. You need forty. Press these open with the seams to the dark side.

ASSEMBLING THE BLOCKS

4. Place your four separate piles of strips, which are in the same order, neatly to the side of your machine next to the pile of four-patch blocks.

5. Take a four-patch block and sew a 4½in strip of the same fabric to either side of it. Press the seams away from the four-patch (see **diagram 4**).

6. Sew an 8½in strip of the same fabric to the top and bottom of this unit (see **diagram 5**). You can chain piece these very quickly so long as you have your piles of fabric in the same order. Make forty blocks. Press the seams away from the four-patch.

ASSEMBLING THE QUILT

7. Referring to **diagram 6**, lay out the blocks into rows, rotating every other block 90 degrees. Make eight rows of five blocks. When you are happy with the layout, sew the blocks into rows and then sew the rows together.

8. Join your six 6½in wide border strips into one continuous length and, referring to Techniques: Adding Borders, add the borders to your quilt.

FINISHING THE QUILT

9. Your quilt top is now complete. Quilt as desired and bind to finish (see Techniques: Quilting and Binding a Quilt).

Interlocking Chains

This striking quilt is quick to piece, but a bit like a jigsaw puzzle when you come to sew the blocks together. However, we've given clear diagrams, so all you need to do is follow them. The quilt looks impressive and is definitely worth the extra attention. Even though our chains are scrappy, it's very important to have two distinct colour groups so the interlocking circles are clearly seen. We used a great jelly roll called Winter Wonderland from Moda that had the perfect mix of reds and whites.

The back of the quilt features a really easy, traditional arrangement of sixteen-patch blocks alternating against a light grey solid.

VITAL STATISTICS

Quilt size: 54in x 66in
Block size: 6in
Number of blocks: 99
Setting: 9 x 11 blocks

REQUIREMENTS

For quilt top:

· One jelly roll OR forty 2½in strips cut across the width of the fabric

· 2½yd (2.25m) background fabric

· 20in (50cm) binding fabric

For pieced quilt back:

· 3yd (2.75m) backing fabric

· Twelve spare jelly roll strips

We chose a quilting design called Modern Beads and kept it dense at the start and end of the quilt and enlarged it towards the centre. The quilt was pieced by the authors and longarm quilted by The Quilt Room.

SORTING THE STRIPS

· You will need to be guided by what is in your jelly roll and artistic licence can be used but it is important to have two distinct colour groups, as follows:

- Fifteen colour A (red) strips

- Thirteen colour B (white) strips

CUTTING INSTRUCTIONS

JELLY ROLL STRIPS COLOUR A (RED)

· Take four colour A strips and cut each strip into sixteen 2½in squares to make a total of sixty-four.

· Take eight colour A strips and cut each strip into eight 2½in x 4½in rectangles to make a total of sixty-four. You need fifty-eight (six are spare).

· Take three colour A strips and cut each strip into six 2½in x 6½in rectangles to make a total of eighteen. You need fourteen (four are spare).

JELLY ROLL STRIPS COLOUR B (WHITE)

· Take four colour B strips and cut each strip into sixteen 2½in squares to make a total of sixty-four.

· Take seven colour B strips and cut each strip into eight 2½in x 4½in rectangles to make a total of fifty-six.

· Take two colour B strips and cut each strip into six 2½in x 6½in rectangles to make a total of twelve. You need eight (four are spare).

BACKGROUND FABRIC

· Cut ten 6½in strips across the width of the fabric. Sub-cut these into fifty-five 6½in squares and four 4½in x 6½in rectangles.

· Cut two 4½in strips across the width of the fabric. Sub-cut these into ten 4½in squares and eight 2½in x 4½in rectangles.

· Cut two 2½in strips across the width of the fabric. Sub-cut these into twenty-two 2½in squares.

BINDING FABRIC

· Cut seven 2½in strips across the width of the fabric.

 Tip

The blade of your rotary cutter will eventually become dull. If you notice that it takes more pressure to cut, or if it misses a few threads when cutting, then it is time to change the blade. You will be amazed at the difference it makes.

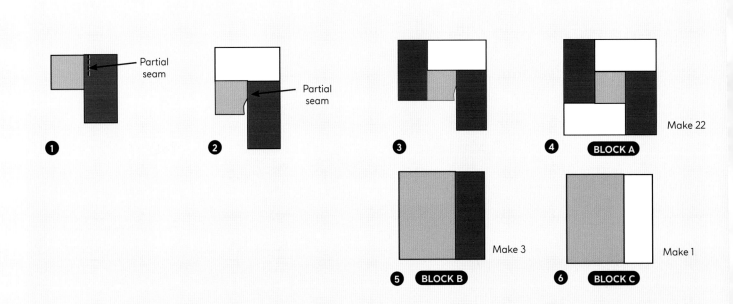

MAKING THE BLOCKS

BLOCK A

1. Take a colour A 2½in x 4½in rectangle and, with right sides together, sew it halfway along a 2½in background square (see **diagram 1**). Press open. The partial seam will be completed after the last rectangle has been sewn on.

2. Sew a colour B 2½in x 4½in rectangle to the top of this unit and press (see **diagram 2**).

3. Sew a colour A 2½in x 4½in rectangle to the left side of this unit and press (see **diagram 3**).

4. Sew a colour B 2½in x 4½in rectangle to the bottom and press. Now complete the partially sewn seam (see **diagram 4, Block A**). Press the seam. Make twenty-two Block A.

BLOCK B

5. Sew a 2½in x 6½in colour A rectangle to a 4½in x 6½in background rectangle (see **diagram 5, Block B**). Make three Block B.

BLOCK C

6. Sew a 2½in x 6½in colour B rectangle to a 4½in x 6½in background rectangle to make one Block C as shown in **diagram 6, Block C**.

BLOCK D

7. Sew a 2½in x 4½in colour A rectangle to a 2½in x 4½in background rectangle and press. Sew a 2½in x 4½in colour B rectangle to the bottom and press (see **diagram 7**).

8. Sew a 2½in x 6½in colour A rectangle on the right-hand side and press (see **diagram 8, Block D**). Make six Block D.

BLOCK E

9. Sew a 2½in x 4½in colour B rectangle to a 2½in x 4½in background rectangle and press. Sew a 2½in x 4½in colour A rectangle to the bottom and press (see **diagram 9**).

10. Sew a 2½in x 6½in colour B rectangle on the right-hand side of the unit to make one Block E and press (see **diagram 10, Block E**).

BLOCK F

11. Sew a 2½in x 4½in colour A rectangle to both sides of a 2½in x 4½in background rectangle and press. Sew a 2½in x 6½in colour B rectangle to the bottom to make one Block F (see **diagram 11, Block F**).

BLOCK G

12. Sew a 2½in x 4½in colour A rectangle to the bottom of a 4½in background square and then sew a 2½in x 6½in colour B rectangle on the right-hand side and press (see **diagram 12, Block G**). Make five Block G.

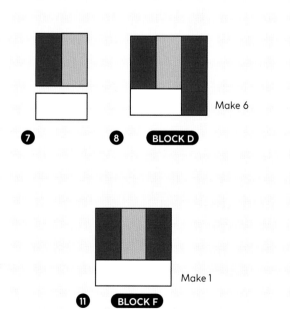

Make 6

7   8   BLOCK D

Make 1

9   10   BLOCK E

Make 1

11   BLOCK F

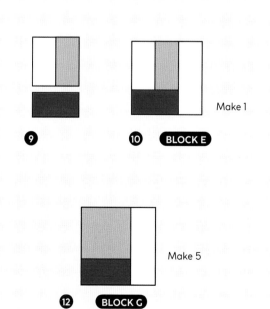

Make 5

12   BLOCK G

BLOCK H

13. Sew a 2½in x 4½in colour B rectangle to the bottom of a 4½in background square and then sew a 2½in x 6½in colour A rectangle to the right-hand side and press. Repeat to make five Block H (see **diagram 13, Block H**).

BLOCK J

14. Draw a diagonal line from corner to corner on the wrong side of a colour A 2½in square, or mark with a fold. With right sides together, lay the marked colour A square on one corner of a 6½in background square, aligning the outer edges. Sew across the diagonal, using the marked diagonal line as the stitching line. Flip the square over and press towards the outside of the block. Trim the excess corner fabric. Don't trim the background square; although this creates a little more bulk, it keeps your work in shape. Repeat on each corner (see **diagram 14, Block J**). Repeat to make ten Block J.

BLOCK K

15. Working with colour B 2½in squares and using the same technique as in step 14, make eight Block K (see **diagram 15, Block K**).

BLOCK L

16. Working with colour A 2½in squares, and sewing only three corners, make six Block L (see **diagram 16, Block L**).

BLOCK M

17. Working with colour B 2½in squares, and sewing only three corners, make four Block M (see **diagram 17, Block M**).

BLOCK N

18. Working with colour A 2½in squares, and sewing only two corners, make two Block N (see **diagram 18, Block N**).

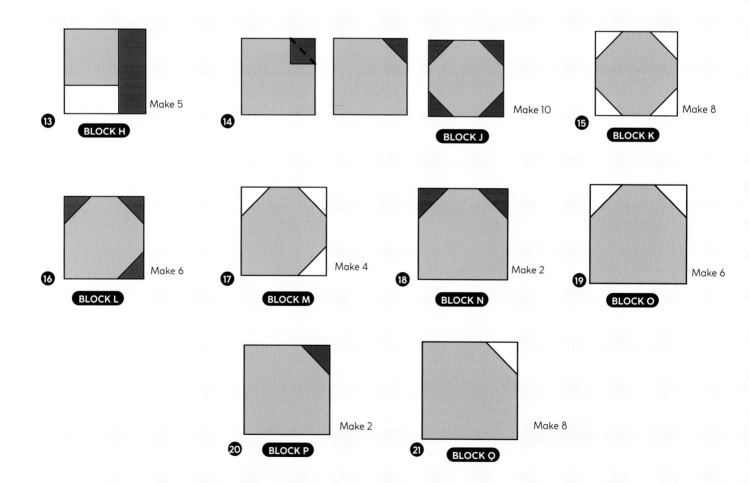

13 BLOCK H — Make 5

14 BLOCK J — Make 10

15 BLOCK K — Make 8

16 BLOCK L — Make 6

17 BLOCK M — Make 4

18 BLOCK N — Make 2

19 BLOCK O — Make 6

20 BLOCK P — Make 2

21 BLOCK Q — Make 8

BLOCK O

19. Working with colour B 2½in squares, and sewing only two corners, make six Block O (see **diagram 19, Block O**).

BLOCK P

20. Working with colour A 2½in squares, and sewing only one corner, make two Block P (see **diagram 20, Block P**).

BLOCK Q

21. Working with colour B 2½in squares, and sewing only one corner, make eight Block Q (see **diagram 21, Block Q**).

ASSEMBLING THE QUILT

22. Refer to **diagram 22** and lay out the blocks into rows. When you are certain that you have everything in the correct place, sew the blocks into rows placing the 6½in background squares where shown on the diagram.

23. Sew the rows together, pinning at every seam intersection to ensure a perfect match.

FINISHING THE QUILT

24. Your quilt top is now complete (see **diagram 23**). You can now make a quilt sandwich as normal with your wadding (batting) and backing fabric, ready for quilting (see Techniques: Quilting). Alternatively, you could piece the back of the quilt as we did by referring to Making a Pieced Quilt Back.

25. After quilting, sew the seven binding strips into a continuous length and bind to finish (see Techniques: Binding a Quilt).

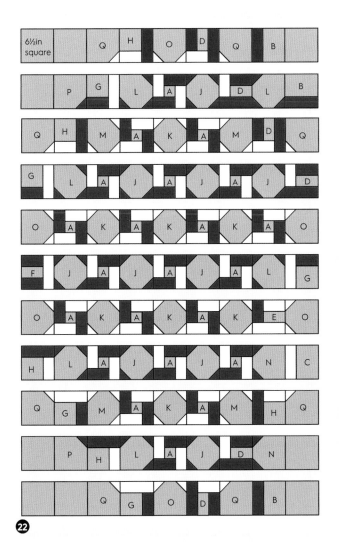

MAKING A PIECED QUILT BACK

CUTTING THE BACKING FABRIC

· Cut three 8½in strips across the width of the fabric and sub-cut two strips into four 8½in squares and cut the third strip into five 8½in squares. You need 42½in to do this so do not trim your selvedge too much. You need thirteen squares in total.

· Cut two 11½in strips across the width of the fabric for the side borders. These need to be 42½in long.

· Cut three 17½in strips across the width of the fabric for the top and bottom borders.

ASSEMBLING THE BACKING

1. Using the twelve jelly roll strips, sew three strip units as shown in **diagram 24** and sub-cut each strip into sixteen 2½in segments to make a total of forty-eight segments.

2. Rotate half the segments 180 degrees and then sew the segments together to form twelve sixteen-patch blocks (see **diagram 25**).

3. Sew the sixteen-patch blocks together with the 8½in background squares to form rows. Sew the rows together, pinning at every seam intersection to ensure a perfect match (see **diagram 26**).

4. Sew on the 11½in wide side borders and press the seams outwards (see **diagram 27**). Sew the three 17½in strips into one continuous length. Trim to size and sew to the top and bottom of the quilt back.

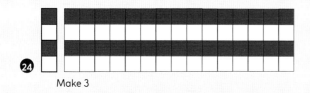

24 Make 3

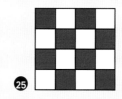

25 Make 12

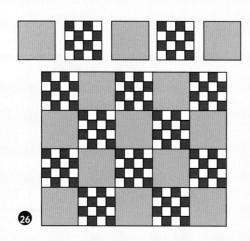

26

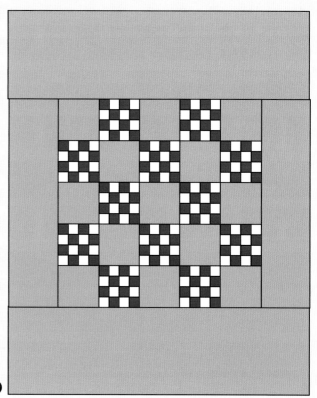

27

The reverse of this quilt uses a much more traditional design and here we have used our jelly roll strips to make some sixteen-patch blocks, setting them against a light grey print. Winter Wonderland from Moda is a very subtle Christmas range and if you look carefully you can see the occasional snowman. The quilt back was pieced by the authors and longarm quilted by The Quilt Room.

Techniques

TOOLS

All the projects in this book require rotary cutting equipment. You will need a self-healing cutting mat at least 18in x 24in and a rotary cutter. We recommend the 45mm or the 60mm diameter cutter. Any rotary cutting work requires rulers and most people have a make they prefer. We like the Creative Grids rulers as their markings are clear, they do not slip on fabric and their Turn-a-Round facility is so useful when dealing with half-inch measurements. We recommend the 6½in x 24in as a basic ruler, plus a large square no less than 12½in, which is handy for squaring up and making sure you are always cutting at right angles.

We have tried not to use too many speciality rulers but when working with 2½in wide strips you do have to re-think some cutting procedures. You will need a speciality ruler to cut half-square triangles which you will find in some of our quilts. Creative Grids have designed the Multi-Size 45/90 ruler for us, which is perfect. Whichever ruler you decide to use, please make sure you are lining up your work on the correct markings. The Creative Grids 45/90 ruler shows the *finished* size measurements. This means that when you are cutting half-square triangles from 2½in strips you must line up the 2in marking along the bottom of the strip. This 2in marking relates to the fact that the finished half-square triangle unit will be 2in. If you are using a different ruler, please make sure you are lining up your work on the correct markings. For example, the Easy Angle ruler shows the *unfinished* size and it will be the 2½in mark that will be lined up with the bottom of the strip.

BASIC TOOL KIT

Some general supplies needed to make the quilts include:

- Tape measure
- Rotary cutter
- Cutting ruler
- Cutting mat
- Scissors
- Needles and pins
- Pencil
- Fabric markers
- Iron
- Sewing machine

SEAMS

We cannot stress enough the importance of maintaining an accurate ¼in seam allowance throughout. We prefer to say an accurate *scant* ¼in seam because there are two factors to take into account. Firstly, the thickness of thread and secondly, when the seam allowance is pressed to one side it takes up a tiny amount of fabric. These are both extremely small amounts but if ignored you'll find your exact ¼in seam allowance is taking up more than ¼in. So, it is worth testing your seam allowance before starting a project. Most sewing machines have various needle positions that can be used to make adjustments.

SEAM ALLOWANCE TEST

Take a 2½in strip and cut off three segments each 1½in wide (see **diagram A**). Sew two segments together down the longer side (see **diagram B**) and press the seam to one side. Sew the third segment across the top (see **diagram C**). It should fit exactly. If it doesn't, you need to make an adjustment to your seam allowance. If it is too long, your seam allowance is too wide and can be corrected by moving the needle on your sewing machine to the right. If it is too small, your seam allowance is too narrow and this can be corrected by moving the needle to the left.

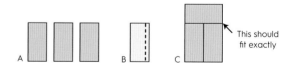

This should fit exactly

PRESSING

In quilt making, pressing is of vital importance and if extra care is taken you will be well rewarded. This is especially true when dealing with strips. If your strips start bowing and stretching you will lose accuracy.

· Always set your seam after sewing by pressing the seam as sewn, without opening up your strips. This eases any tension and prevents the seam line from distorting. Move the iron with an up and down motion, zigzagging along the seam rather than ironing down the length of the seam, which could cause distortion.

· Open up your strips and press on the *right* side of the fabric towards the darker fabric, if necessary guiding the seam underneath to make sure the seam is going in the right direction. Press with an up and down motion rather than along the length of the strip.

· Always take care if using steam and certainly don't use steam anywhere near a bias edge.

· Each seam must be pressed flat before another seam is sewn across it. Unless there is a special reason for not doing so, seams are pressed towards the darker fabric. The main criteria when joining seams, however, is to have the seam allowances going in the opposite direction to each other as they then nest together without bulk. Your patchwork will lie flat and your seam intersections will be accurate.

PINNING

Don't underestimate the benefits of pinning. When you have to align a seam, it is important to insert pins to stop any movement when sewing. Long, fine pins with flat heads are recommended as they will go through the layers of fabric easily and allow you to sew up to and over them. Seams should always be pressed in opposite directions so they will nest together nicely. Insert a pin either at right angles or diagonally through the seam intersection ensuring that the seams are matching perfectly. When sewing, do not remove the pin too early as your fabric might shift and your seams will not be perfectly aligned.

CHAIN PIECING

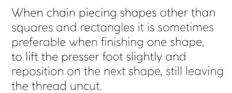

Chain piecing is the technique of feeding a series of pieces through the sewing machine without lifting the presser foot and without cutting the thread between each piece. Always chain piece when you can as it saves both time and thread. Once your chain is complete simply snip the thread between pieces.

When chain piecing shapes other than squares and rectangles it is sometimes preferable when finishing one shape, to lift the presser foot slightly and reposition on the next shape, still leaving the thread uncut.

REMOVING DOG EARS

A dog ear is the excess piece of fabric that overlaps past the seam allowance when sewing triangles to other shapes. Dog ears should always be cut off to reduce bulk. They can be trimmed using a rotary cutter although snipping with small, sharp scissors is quicker. Make sure you are trimming the points parallel to the straight edge of the triangle.

JOINING BORDER AND BINDING STRIPS

If you need to join strips for your borders and binding, you may choose to join them with a diagonal seam to make them less noticeable. If you do this, be aware that the amount of fabric lost in the seam allowance is more than for straight seams. Place the strips right sides together, at a 90-degree angle as shown in **diagram A**, and sew a diagonal seam. Press the seam open (see **diagram B**).

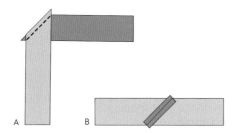

ADDING BORDERS

The fabric requirements in this book all assume you are going to be sewing straight rather than mitred borders. If you intend to have mitred borders please add sufficient extra fabric for this. In the quilts described we have given the length that you need to cut border strips, but it's a good idea to wait until your quilt centre is made and then check your measurements before cutting.

ADDING STRAIGHT BORDERS

1. Determine the vertical measurement from top to bottom through the centre of your quilt top. Cut two side border strips to this measurement. Mark the halves and quarters of one quilt side and one border with pins. Placing right sides together and matching the pins, stitch the quilt and border together, easing the quilt side to fit where necessary. Repeat on the opposite side. Press open.

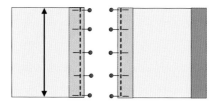

2. Determine the horizontal measurement from side to side across the centre of the quilt top. Cut two top and bottom border strips to this measurement and add to the quilt top in the same manner as before.

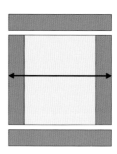

QUILTING

Quilting stitches hold the patchwork top, wadding (batting) and backing together and create texture over your finished patchwork. The choice is yours whether you hand quilt, machine quilt or send it off to a longarm quilting service. There are many books dedicated to the techniques of hand and machine quilting but the basic procedure is as follows:

1. With the aid of templates or a ruler, mark out the quilting lines on the patchwork top.

2. Cut the backing fabric and wadding (batting) at least 4in larger all around than the patchwork top. Pin or tack (baste) the layers together to prepare them for quilting.

3. Quilt either by hand or by machine. Remove any quilting marks or tacking (basting) after quilting.

BINDING A QUILT

The binding used in this book is a 2½in double-fold binding cut on the straight grain.

1. Trim the excess backing and wadding (batting) so that the edges are even with the top of the quilt.

2. Join your binding strips into a continuous length, making sure there is sufficient to go around the quilt plus 8in–10in for corners and overlapping ends. With wrong sides together, press the binding in half lengthways. Fold and press under ½in to neaten the edge at the end where you will start sewing.

3. On the right side of the quilt and starting about 12in away from a corner, align the edges of the double thickness binding with the edge of the quilt, so that the cut edges are towards the edges of the quilt, and pin to hold in place. Sew with a ¼in seam allowance, leaving the first few inches open.

4. At the first corner, stop ¼in from the edge of the fabric and backstitch (see **diagram A**). Lift the needle and presser foot and fold the binding upwards (see **diagram B**). Fold the binding again but downwards. Stitch from the edge to ¼in from the next corner (see **diagram C**).

5. Repeat the corner mitring process and continue on all around the quilt working each corner in the same way. When you come back to the starting point, cut the binding, fold under the cut edge and overlap at the starting point.

6. Fold the binding over to the back of the quilt and hand stitch in place, folding the binding at each corner to form a neat mitre.

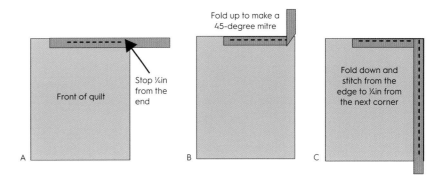

A — Front of quilt / Stop ¼in from the end

B — Fold up to make a 45-degree mitre

C — Fold down and stitch from the edge to ¼in from the next corner

MAKING A LARGER QUILT

If you want to make a larger version of any of the quilts in the book, refer to the Vital Statistics of the quilt, which generally give information such as the block size, the number of blocks, how the blocks are set plus the size of border used. You can then calculate your requirements for a larger quilt.

SETTING ON POINT

Any block can take on a totally new look when set on point and you might like to try one of the quilts to see what it looks like with this arrangement. For this reason we have included information here for setting quilts on point. Some people are a little daunted as there are a few things to take into consideration but here are the basics.

HOW WIDE WILL BLOCKS BE WHEN SET ON POINT?

To calculate the measurement of the block from point to point, multiply the size of the finished block by 1.414. Example: a 12in block will measure 12in x 1.414 which is 16.97in – just under 17in diagonally. Now you can calculate how many blocks you need for your quilt.

HOW DO I PIECE BLOCKS ON POINT?

Piece rows diagonally, starting at a corner. Triangles have to be added to the end of each row before joining the rows and these are called setting triangles. To finish, corner triangles need to be added to square off the corners of the quilt.

HOW DO I CALCULATE WHAT SIZE SETTING TRIANGLES TO CUT?

Setting triangles form the outside of your quilt and need to have the straight grain of the fabric on the outside edge, to prevent stretching. To ensure this, these triangles are formed from quarter-square triangles, i.e., a square cut into four. The measurement for this is: Finished Diagonal Block Size + 1¼in. Example: a 12in block (diagonal measurement approximately 17in) should be 18¼in.

Corner triangles are added last. They also need to have the outside edge on the straight grain, so these should be cut from half-square triangles. To calculate the size of square to cut in half, divide the finished size of your block by 1.414 then add ⅞in. Example: a 12in block would be 12in divided by 1.414 = 8.49in + ⅞in (0.88) = 9.37in (or 9½in as it can be trimmed later).

Most diagonal quilts start off with one block and in each row thereafter the number of blocks increases by two. All rows contain an odd number of blocks. To calculate the finished size of the quilt, you count the number of diagonals across and multiply this by the diagonal measurement of the block. Do the same with the number of blocks down and multiply this by the diagonal measurement of the block.

If you want a rectangular quilt instead of a square one, you count the number of blocks in the row that establishes the width and repeat that number in following rows until the desired length is established.

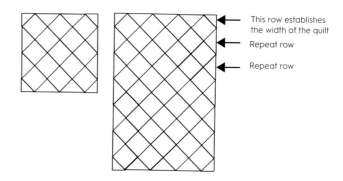

This row establishes the width of the quilt

Repeat row

Repeat row

CALCULATING BACKING FABRIC

The patterns in this book do not include fabric requirements for backing as many people like to use extra-wide backing fabric so they do not have to have any joins.

USING 60IN WIDE FABRIC

This is a simple calculation as to how much you need to buy. Example: your quilt is 54in x 72in. Your backing needs to be 3in larger all round so your backing measurement is 60in x 78in. If you have found 60in wide backing, then you would buy the length which is 78in. However, if you have found 90in wide backing, you can turn it round and you would only have to buy 60in (i.e., the width of the quilt).

USING 42IN WIDE FABRIC

If using this width, you will need to have a join or joins in order to get the required measurement unless the backing measurement for your quilt is 42in or less on one side. If your backing measurement is less than 42in then you need only buy one length.

Using the previous example, if your backing measurement is 60in x 78in, you will have to have one seam somewhere in your backing. If you join two lengths of 42in fabric together your new fabric measurement will be 84in (less a little for the seam). This would be sufficient for the length of your quilt so you need to buy two times the width, i.e., 60in x 2 = 120in. Your seam will run horizontally.

If your quilt length is more than your new backing fabric measurement of 84in, you will need to use the 84in measurement for the width of the quilt and you will have to buy two times the length. Your seam will then run vertically.

LABELLING A QUILT

When you have finished your quilt it is important to label it even if the information you put on the label is just your name and the date. When looking at antique quilts it is always interesting to piece together information about the quilt, and any extra information you put on the label will be of immense interest to future quilters. For example, you could say why you made the quilt and who it was for, or for what special occasion. Labels can be as ornate as you like, but a simple and quick method is to write on a piece of calico with a permanent marker pen and then appliqué this to the back of your quilt.

ABOUT THE AUTHORS

Pam Lintott opened her quilt shop, The Quilt Room, in 1981, which she still runs today, along with her daughter Nicky. In 2021 they celebrated forty years from the shop's opening – the oldest quilt shop in the UK. Pam is the author of *The Quilt Room Patchwork & Quilting Workshops*, as well as *The Quilter's Workbook*, in addition to having authored many titles with Nicky. In 2018 they relocated their shop to outside Dorking town, which has the advantage of having plenty of parking, plus longarm machines, mail-order department, workshop studio and shop, all under one roof. It makes for a very happy environment.

OTHER BOOKS FROM THE AUTHORS

 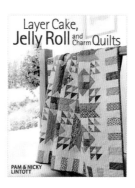 

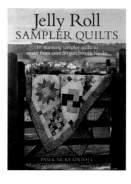 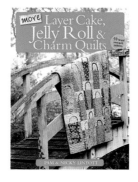 

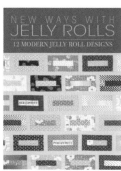  

USEFUL CONTACTS

THE QUILT ROOM

Shop & Mail Order

7–9, Beare Green Court,
Old Horsham Road,
Beare Green,
Dorking RH5 4QU, UK
Tel: 01306 877307
www.quiltroom.co.uk

MODA FABRICS/UNITED NOTIONS

13800 Hutton Drive,
Dallas, Texas 75234, USA
Tel: 800-527-9447
www.modafabrics.com

CREATIVE GRIDS (UK) LTD

23A Pate Road,
Melton Mowbray, Leicestershire
LE13 0RG, UK
Tel: 01664 501724
www.creativegrids.com

JANOME UK LTD

Janome Centre,
Southside, Stockport,
Cheshire SK6 2SP, UK
Tel: 0161 666 6011
www.janome.com

ACKNOWLEDGEMENTS

Pam and Nicky would firstly like to thank Moda Fabrics for their inspirational idea of jelly rolls, for their continued support in all they do, and for allowing them to use the name jelly roll in the title and throughout the book.

They would also like to thank David and Charles for producing such beautiful books. Their photography is second to none and they really appreciate their attention to detail.

They would also like to thank their husbands, Nick and Rob, for their continued love and support over the years.

Index

A DAVID AND CHARLES BOOK
© David and Charles, Ltd 2023

David and Charles is an imprint of David and Charles, Ltd
Suite A, Tourism House, Pynes Hill, Exeter, EX2 5WS

Text and Designs © Pam and Nicky Lintott 2023
Layout and Photography © David and Charles, Ltd 2023

First published in the UK and USA in 2023
Content previously published in: *Jelly Roll Quilts*; *Layer Cake, Jelly Roll and Charm Quilts*; *Two From One Jelly Roll Quilts*; *More Layer Cake, Jelly Roll and Charm Quilts*; *Antique to Heirloom Jelly Roll Quilts*; *Jelly Roll Quilts in a Weekend*; *Jelly Roll Quilts The Classic Collection*; and *New Ways With Jelly Roll Quilts*.

Pam and Nicky Lintott have asserted their right to be identified as authors of this work in accordance with the Copyright, Designs and Patents Act, 1988.

A catalogue record for this book is available from the British Library.

ISBN-13: 9781446309711 paperback
ISBN-13: 9781446382363 EPUB
ISBN-13: 9781446310434 PDF

This book has been printed on paper from approved suppliers and made from pulp from sustainable sources.

Printed in Turkey by Omur for:
David and Charles, Ltd
Suite A, Tourism House, Pynes Hill, Exeter, EX2 5WS

10 9 8 7 6 5 4 3 2 1

Publishing Director: Ame Verso
Senior Commissioning Editor: Sarah Callard
Managing Editor: Jeni Chown
Editor: Jessica Cropper
Project Editors: Linda Clements and Cheryl Brown
Head of Design: Anna Wade
Designers: Sam Staddon and Blanche Williams
Pre-press Designer: Ali Stark
Illustrations: Linda Clements and Ethan Danielson
Art Direction: Prudence Rogers and Laura Woussen
Photography: Jason Jenkins, Lorna Yabsley, Kim Sayer, Karl Adamson, Sian Irvine, Joe Giacomet, Jack Kirby and Jack Gorman
Production Manager: Beverley Richardson

David and Charles publishes high-quality books on a wide range of subjects. For more information visit www.davidandcharles.com.

Share your makes with us on social media using #dandcbooks and follow us on Facebook and Instagram by searching for @dandcbooks.

Layout of the digital edition of this book may vary depending on reader hardware and display settings.